FAST TRACK ENGLISH

Helping Hands

Grammar & Exercises

Robert Parr

with

Günther Albrecht

TR-Verlagsunion

Die Deutsche Bibliothek – CIP-Einheitsaufnahme

Fast track English / Robert Parr with Günther Albrecht. – München : TR-Verl.-Union.

Helping hands : grammar & exercises
Buch. – 1997
ISBN 3-8058-3250-8

Zu *Helping Hands* gibt es eine **Übungskassette** (Best.-Nr. 32516). Die auf Band wiedergegebenen Übungen aus dem Buch sind jeweils durch das Symbol ●● gekennzeichnet.

Literaturnachweis:

A Spanish Lover © Joanna Trollope (Black Swan, 1993); *Cider with Rosie* © Laurie Lee (Penguin, 1962); *For Whom the Bell Tolls* © Ernest Hemingway (Grafton Books, 1976); *Goodbye to All That* © Robert Graves (Penguin, 1960); *High Fidelity* © Nick Hornby (Indigo, 1995); *Hotel du Lac* © Anita Brookner (Triad/Panther, 1984); *Jill* © Philip Larkin (Faber & Faber, 1975); *Man from the South* in 'Completely Unexpected Tales' © Roald Dahl (Penguin, 1986); *Martha Quest* © Doris Lessing (Granada, 1966); *Parkinson's Law* © C. Northcote Parkinson (John Murray, 1954); *The Garden Party* © Katherine Mansfield (Penguin, 1951); *The Way up to Heaven* in 'Completely Unexpected Tales' © Roald Dahl (Penguin, 1986)

4. Auflage 2002

Umschlaggestaltung: Franziska Schob-Bergmeir, München
Gesamtherstellung: Druckerei Bremberger, München
ISBN 3-8058-3250-8

VORWORT

Grammatik bietet Konfliktstoff. Die einen behaupten, erst mit Grammatik könne eine Sprache beherrscht werden. Die anderen betonen, trotz unsicherer Grammatikkenntnisse verstanden zu werden, was viel wichtiger sei.

Grammatik ist ein elementares Gerüst. Ohne ihre sichere Beherrschung und einen gut entwickelten Wortschatz fällt es dem Lernenden schwer, seine Sprachkenntnisse auszubauen. Grammatik hat nicht nur mit Regeln, sondern, zusammen mit dem Wortschatz, v.a. auch mit effektiver Kommunikation zu tun.

Grammatik markiert wesentliche Bedeutungsunterschiede. Ein Beispiel:

Victoria and Theresa have been here for an hour.
Victoria and Theresa are here for an hour.

Im ersten Satz sind beide Damen schon seit einer Stunde da. Im zweiten Satz werden sie, ab jetzt, eine Stunde hier sein.

Helping Hands – Grammar & Exercises versucht einen Ausgleich zwischen Überbewerten und Unterschätzen der englischen Grammatik.

Jede Lektion besteht aus einer Doppelseite. Die linke Seite stellt, auf Deutsch, Grundzüge der englischen Grammatik in übersichtlichen Schaubildern und knappen Worten dar. Auf der rechten Seite folgt, in englischer Sprache, ein bunter Übungsteil. Einige Übungen sind traditioneller Art: Lückentexte, Umformulierungen, auch kleine Übersetzungen. Andere, v.a. die sog. *concept questions*, sollen zum Nachdenken über Strukturen anregen. Auszüge aus bekannten Romanen lassen Englisch nicht nur in einzelnen Sätze, sondern auch im Kontext genießen. Zu allen Übungen gibt es im Anhang die Lösungen.

Helping Hands – Grammar & Exercises ist also Kurzgrammatik, Übungsheft und Unterhaltung zugleich. Der Aufbau des Buchs gestattet, je nach Vorkenntnissen, Zeit oder auch Laune, einen flexiblen Umgang beim Lernen und Üben.

Good luck and all the best!

Robert Parr, Günther Albrecht

INHALT

1. Der unbestimmte Artikel 8
2. Der bestimmte Artikel 10
3. Die Mehrzahl des Substantivs 12
4. Besonderheiten bei der Mehrzahlbildung 14
5. Der Genitiv 16
6. Personalpronomen 18
7. Possessivpronomen, Reflexivpronomen, Pronomen der Gegenseitigkeit . 20
8. Fragepronomen, Demonstrativpronomen 22
9. Relativpronomen 24
10. Mengenbezeichnungen 26
11. Adjektive 28
12. Adverbien 30
13. Präpositionen und Konjunktionen 32
14. Primäre Hilfsverben 34
15. Modale Hilfsverben I 36
16. Modale Hilfsverben II 38
17. Modale Hilfsverben III 40
18. Modale Hilfsverben IV 42
19. Modale Hilfsverben V 44
20. Ersatzformen für Hilfsverben 46
21. Andere Hilfsverben 48
22. 'have' & 'have got' 50
23. Frage, Frageanhängsel, Kurzantwort 52
24. Verbformen 54
25. Die einfache Form der Gegenwart 56
26. Die Verlaufsform der Gegenwart 58
27. Die einfache Form der Vergangenheit 60
28. Die Verlaufsform der Vergangenheit 62
29. Die einfache Form des Perfekts 64
30. Die Verlaufsform des Perfekts 66
31. Die einfache Form der Vorvergangenheit 68
32. Die Verlaufsform der Vorvergangenheit 70
33. Zustandsverben 72
34. Zukunftsformen I 74
35. Zukunftsformen II 76
36. 'going to' & 'will' + Infinitiv 78
37. Gegenwartsformen für Zukunftsereignisse 80

38. Das Passiv ... 82
39. Entsprechungen für ‚lassen' ... 84
40. Zusammengesetzte Verben ... 86
41. Das Verb und seine Ergänzungen ... 88
42. If-Sätze ... 90
43. 'I wish ...' ... 92
44. Indirekte Rede I ... 94
45. Indirekte Rede II ... 96
46. Relativsätze ... 98
47. Das Gerund ... 100
48. Der Infinitiv ... 102
49. Gerund oder Infinitiv ... 104
50. Das Partizip Präsens ... 106
51. Das Partizip Perfekt ... 108
52. Nebensätze ... 110
53. Amerikanisches Englisch ... 112
54. Zahlen ... 114
55. Datum und Uhrzeit ... 116

Lösungen ... 119

Unregelmäßige Verben ... 133

Grammatische Begriffe ... 136

Register ... 140

'The question is,' said Alice, 'whether you can make words mean different things.' 'The question is,' said Humpty Dumpty, 'which is to be master – that's all.'

Alice was much too puzzled to say anything, so after a minute Humpty Dumpty began again. 'They've a temper most of them – particularly verbs, they're the proudest – adjectives you can anything do with, but not verbs – however, I can manage the whole lot!'

From *Through the Looking-Glass* by Lewis Carroll.

1 Der unbestimmte Artikel (The indefinite article)

Der unbestimmte Artikel lautet **'a'** /ə/ vor Wörtern, die in der Aussprache mit einem **Konsonanten** beginnen, und **'an'** /ən/ vor Wörtern, die mit einem **Vokal** anlauten, z.B.

a	*car* *building* *dog* *newspaper* *university* /ˌjuː.../ *one-way street* /ˌwʌn'.../	***an***	*apple* *egg* *office* *hour* /ˈaʊeʳ/ *animal* *operation*

- Der unbestimmte Artikel steht **nach 'to be', 'to become'** und **'as'** bei Angaben zu **Beruf, Nationalität** und **Religion,** z.B.

  He's a student.
  She wants to become an engineer.
  She's working as a computer programmer.

  Auch bei Angaben zu **Preis, Häufigkeit** und **Geschwindigkeit** benutzt man den unbestimmten Artikel im Englischen, z.B.

  Oranges cost over £1.90 a pound.
  We see each other four times a week.
  This train goes over 180 miles an hour.

  Der unbestimmte Artikel findet sich in **feststehenden Ausdrücken,** wie z.B.

to be in a hurry	
to have a headache	(aber: *to have toothache*)
to have a drink	
it's a pity that	
for a change	(zur Abwechslung)
as a rule	(in der Regel)

- Bei **nicht zählbaren Substantiven** wie 'information', 'advice', 'chewing gum', 'news' etc. (s. unit 4) steht **nie 'a'** oder **'an'.** Für Mengenangaben verwendet man **stattdessen 'a piece of', 'an item of'** oder **'a bit of',** z.B.

  Would you like a piece of chewing gum? (... einen Kaugummi?)
  Here is an interesting bit of news. (... eine ... Nachricht.)

1 Exercises

I. Add 'a' or 'an' to complete the sentences. ●●

1. Would you like … piece of fruit? … banana, … apple?
2. The flight to London takes about … hour and … half.
3. Do all British children have to wear … uniform at school?
4. We've got … new telephone number. It's … easy one to remember.
5. Is English really … international language?
6. Is Green Park the name of … Underground station in London?
7. … uncle of mine lives in Florida. He's become … US citizen.
8. My sister wants to become … actress when she's older.

II. Put 'a' or 'an' into the gaps to complete the sentences. ●●

1. Mary-Jo's … American and not … Canadian, isn't she?
2. He was ... engineer before he became … computer specialist.
3. Is the new US president … Republican or … Democrat?
4. He's working as … sales assistant during the summer holidays.
5. Is he married? - No, he's still … bachelor.
6. Do you say 'he's English' or 'he's … Englishman'? - Both.
7. She's training to be … lawyer in the States. - Don't they say … 'attorney' in the USA?
8. Is Malcolm … Scot? - Yes, can't you hear that he's got … Glaswegian accent?

*III. What's their line (*Branche*)? Write down what these people's jobs are.*

1. Andrew writes articles for newspapers and magazines. He's … .
2. Cathy looks after people in hospital. She's … .
3. Mike flies planes. He's … .
4. Sally works in a school where she teaches Maths. She's … .
5. Rupert cuts people's hair. He's … .
6. Jane plays the violin in an orchestra. She's … .

IV. Translate these sentences into English making sure you use the indefinite article correctly.

1. Ich gehe dreimal pro Woche zum Schwimmen.
2. Zucker kostet £1.70 das Kilo.
3. Es ist schade, dass sie nicht kommen kann.
4. Können Sie mir einen Rat geben?

2 Der bestimmte Artikel (The definite article)

Der bestimmte Artikel wird im Englischen seltener verwendet als im Deutschen; **'the'** lautet /ðə/ vor Konsonanten und /ði/ vor Vokalen, z. B.

	house			*advice*	
the /ðə/	*European Union*	(/j/-Laut)	***the*** /ði/	*excitement*	
	one I like best	(/w/-Laut)		*hour*	(stummes 'h')

- **Abstrakte Begriffe** stehen i. d. R. **ohne 'the',** z. B.

  Such is life. *What do you think of politics?*

  Auch bei **Zeitangaben,** wie Wochentagen, Monaten, Jahreszeiten und Festtagen, entfällt der bestimmte Artikel, z. B.

  Summer is my favourite part of the year.
  What are you doing at Christmas?

  Der bestimmte Artikel entfällt ebenfalls bei **Institutionen** und **Einrichtungen,** wenn von ihrer **Hauptfunktion** die Rede ist, z. B.

  to be at school *(as a pupil)*
  to spend a night in hospital *(as a patient)*

  Vor **Mahlzeiten** steht meist kein Artikel, z. B.

  When is lunch ready? *What's for dinner tonight?*

- Wenn aber Begriffe wie 'life', 'summer' oder 'school' durch einen Zusatz **näher erläutert** werden, verwendet man **'the',** z. B.

  The life she's leading at the moment must be very tiring.
  The hospital my grandfather's in has an excellent reputation.

- Einige, aber nicht alle bekannten **Straßen- und Gebäudenamen** bleiben in der Einzahl ohne Artikel, z. B.

Oxford Street	**aber:**	*the World Trade Center*
Buckingham Palace		*the Tate Gallery*
Central Park		*the Golden Gate Bridge*
Fifth Avenue		*the British Museum*

2 Exercises

I. To complete these sentences add 'the' where it is necessary.

1. John broke his leg during a football match and he's now in … hospital.
2. Who makes … breakfast in your house? You or your wife?
3. Do you normally go away at … Whitsun (*Pfingsten*)?
4. Is … Turkey in … European Union?
5. When we were in London we went to … Trafalgar Square but we didn't go into … National Gallery.
6. What did you do at … school today, Victoria?
7. 'Can … death be sleep if … life is but (*nur*) a dream?' (*John Keats*)
8. My favourite month of … year is … May.

II. Read these sentences carefully. Where do you need a 'the'? ●●

1. Is your daughter still at … school?
2. We don't like … Christmas. It's so commercial.
3. Anna hopes to go to … university to study Engineering.
4. Can you see the smoke over there! There's a fire at … school!
5. This year the conference will be held at … university in Canterbury.
6. Are you religious? Do you go to … church every week?
7. Five years ago he robbed a bank and he's been in … prison ever since.
8. Where's the second-hand book sale? – In … church.

III. Places of interest in London. You need 'the' three times. But where? ●●

1. … Westminster Abbey is not far from … Houses of Parliament.
2. London's most famous sight is … Buckingham Palace.
3. Many people find … Oxford Street very busy. … Strand is quieter.
4. To get to … Windsor Castle you can go by train from … Paddington Station.
5. In … Soho there are lots of places to eat. Remember that restaurants in … West End are often extremely expensive.
6. When you've had enough of all the people go and relax in … Hyde Park.

IV. Try and translate the following into English.

1. Zum Frieden gibt es keine Alternative.
2. Der Tod ist ein notwendiges Ende.
3. Das Leben kann so schön sein.
4. Die moderne Gesellschaft denkt anders.

3 Die Mehrzahl des Substantivs (The plural of nouns)

Das englische Substantiv wird i.d.R. **klein** geschrieben. **Ausnahmen: Eigennamen, Länder, Wochentage, Monate, Orte,** z.B.

Is Alex from Germany?
The conference begins on Wednesday, 9 December.

- Die Mehrzahl des Substantivs wird meist durch **Anhängen von -s** an die Einzahl gebildet, z.B.

book	*books*	*cup*	*cups*

- Bei Substantiven, die in der Einzahl auf **-s, -ss, -sh, -ch** oder **-x** enden, bildet man die Mehrzahl durch **Anhängen von -es,** z.B.

church	*churches*	*bus*	*buses*

- Bei Substantiven, die mit **-y nach einem Konsonanten** enden, wird aus dem -y in der Einzahl **-ies** in der Mehrzahl, z.B.

baby	*babies*	*story*	*stories*

Bei **-y nach einem Vokal** wird ein **-s angehängt,** z.B.

day	*days*	*boy*	*boys*

- Substantive, die auf **-f** oder **-fe** enden, bilden die Mehrzahl mit **-ves,** z.B.

knife *knives* *shelf* *shelves* (aber: *roof* *roofs*)

- **Unregelmäßige Mehrzahlbildungen:**

man	***men***	*foot*	***feet***
woman	***women*** /ˈwɪmɪn/	*tooth*	***teeth***
child	***children***	*tomato*	***tomatoes***
person	***people***	*sheep*	***sheep***

- Bei der Mehrzahlbildung **unbekannter oder ungewöhnlicher Wörter** empfiehlt es sich, in einem guten einsprachigen Wörterbuch nachzuschlagen, z.B.

phenomenon	*phenomena*	*grown-up*	*grown-ups*
crisis	*crises*	*son-in-law*	*sons-in-law*

3 Exercises

I. Complete the sentences by putting the words in brackets into their plural form.

1. Good morning, (lady) and (gentleman)! And good morning (child)!
2. Are London's telephone (box) red and its (taxi) black?
3. How many (woman) have top (job) in business?
4. Are (lorry) allowed to drive along narrow (street) like these?
5. Over 500 (person) work in our (office).
6. You can have three (wish)!
7. Are (orange) more expensive than (strawberry) at the moment?
8. Do you like going to (party)?

II. Turn the singular forms into plural forms and the plural forms into singular forms.

1. Is this your tomato?
2. She's a young child.
3. A Dublin bus is green.
4. There's not one leaf on that tree.
5. Discos are fantastic!
6. Do your teeth hurt?
7. Men can't have babies.
8. You left your books on my shelves.

III. Look up (or work out) these difficult plural forms.

1. mother-in-law
2. sheep
3. woman driver
4. life
5. analysis

IV. Put the words in brackets into the plural. ●●

Water was the most active thing in the valley, arriving in the long rains from Wales. It would drop all day from (cloud) and (tree), from (roof) and eaves (*Dachvorsprüngen*) and (nose). It broke open (road), carved (*bahnte sich*) its way through (garden), and filled the (ditch, *Graben*) with sucking (noise).

(From *Cider with Rosie* by Laurie Lee)

4 Besonderheiten bei der Mehrzahlbildung (Special points to note with the plural)

- Es gibt eine Reihe von Substantiven im Englischen, die nur in der **Mehrzahl** vorkommen. Meist sind es **Kleidungsstücke** wie 'shorts', 'jeans' und 'leggings' oder **Werkzeuge** wie 'scissors', 'scales' (*Waage*) und 'pliers' (*Zange*), die aus **zwei Teilen** bestehen. Das zugehörige **Verb/Pronomen** steht in der **Mehrzahl,** z. B.

  Where are my shorts?
  These jeans have shrunk!
  Are these your scissors or mine?
  These scales aren't working properly.

- Einige gebräuchliche Substantive im Englischen sind, im Gegensatz zum Deutschen, **nicht zählbar,** wie 'information', 'advice', 'hair', 'weather', 'research', 'news', 'progress', 'furniture' und 'traffic' (s. unit 1). Diese Substantive haben **keine Mehrzahl** und kommen **ohne den unbestimmten Artikel** in der Einzahl vor. Um eine unbestimmte Menge auszudrücken, verwendet man i. d. R. **'some',** z. B.

  We've got some information for you.
  Can you give me some advice?
  Is my hair too long?
  What lovely weather!

- Obwohl Substantive wie 'the United States', 'the Netherlands', 'mathematics', 'aerobics', 'darts', 'news', 'data' und 'media' **Pluralendungen** haben, werden sie i. d. R. als **Einheit** aufgefasst. Das **Verb** steht in der **Einzahl,** z. B.

  The USA supports the prime minister's decision.
  Is the data available yet?
  Has darts become a popular game in your country?

- Bei Gruppenbezeichnungen wie 'family', 'team', 'class', 'audience' und 'government' ist entscheidend, ob man die **Gruppe als Einheit ('it')** ***oder*** **als Einzelpersonen ('they')** betrachtet, z. B.

  How's the family?
  The team have not played very well.

4 Exercises

I. Choose the correct word in each pair of brackets to complete the sentences. ●●

1. Would you like (a/some) chewing gum?
2. We had (a/some) difficult homework last weekend, didn't we?
3. Your furniture (is/are) very nice. Did you buy (it/them) recently?
4. Our luggage (isn't/aren't) here so it probably (hasn't/haven't) come off the plane.

II. Complete the questions by using 'is' or 'are', 'does' or 'do', 'has' or 'have'.

1. … the Netherlands in the European Union?
2. … the United Nations meet in New York?
3. … the media only interested in sensational stories?
4. … the data been collected?

III. Translate the following sentences into English.

1. Die Informationen, die wir über Irland erhielten, waren sehr interessant.
2. Er braucht eine neue Brille.
3. Vielen Dank für die Ratschläge, die Sie uns gegeben haben.
4. Möchtest du noch einen Toast oder noch ein Stück Kuchen?

IV. Which sentence on the right (a or b) is an appropriate response to the question on the left?

1. How's my English?	a. You're making a lot of progresses. b. You're making a lot of progress.
2. Why is she crying?	a. There was some bad news. b. There were bad news.

V. Look up the following noun in a good dictionary. What is difficult about it for learners of English? How is it used correctly? Write down an example sentence.

police

5 Der Genitiv (The genitive)

- Der sog. **'s-genitive'** steht **vor** dem zugehörigen Substantiv. Er wird bei **Personen, Tieren** und oft auch bei **Ländern, Städten** und **Zeitbestimmungen** verwendet, z.B.

  a woman's problem *London's nightlife*
  a dog's life *last week's lesson*
  South America's cities *yesterday's weather*

  Der **'s-genitive'** erhält in der **Einzahl** die Endung **-'s,** z.B.

  my brother's car *the lady's bag*

  In der **Mehrzahl** erhalten Substantive mit Mehrzahl-s ein **Apostroph ',** Substantive ohne Mehrzahl-s die Endung **-'s,** z.B.

  my friends' computers *the men's toilets*
  a boys' jacket *children's toys*

a woman	**'s**	bag	my friends	**'**	bikes	some men	**'s**	clothes

- Der sog. **'shop apostrophe'** wird bei **öffentlichen Gebäuden** und **Läden** verwendet, wobei das Wort **'shop', 'house', 'store' entfällt,** z.B.

  Where's the nearest chemist's (shop)?
  We were in St. Mary's (church).

- Das **Besitzwort entfällt,** wo es verzichtbar ist, z.B.

  Whose bag is this? – It's John's (bag).
  Excuse me. Where's the ladies' (room), please?

- Der sog. **'of-genitive'** steht **nach** dem zugehörigen Substanitv. Er wird i.d.R. bei **Sachen** verwendet, z.B.

  the end of the road *the age of technology*

  Auch bei **(Mengen-)Angaben** wie den folgenden verwendet man 'of':

a box of *chocolates*	***a tin of*** *soup*	
a packet of *cigarettes*	***a pile of*** *paper*	
a jar of *jam*	***a tube of*** *toothpaste*	(aber: *a dozen eggs*)

5 Exercises

I. What is needed to complete these sentences?

1. Chris … family lives near Bath.
2. The ladies … department is on the ground floor.
3. Are these men … trousers or boy …?
4. His brother … name … are Craig and Rick.
5. St. James … Park is opposite Buckingham Palace.
6. These must be children … bikes. They're so small.
7. I'm just going to the doctor … . I'll be back soon.
8. Was that your idea or your parent …?

II. Rewrite the following sentences. Use an 's structure where the words are underlined.

1. Exports from Germany to the rest of Europe have not increased.
2. And now the results of the football matches this evening.
3. The population of the world is rising dramatically.
4. The largest city in England after London is Birmingham.
5. Did you read the *Times* from last Saturday?
6. The success of the company depends on all the employees.

III. Write out these sentences in full. In five of the sentences you must use an 'of'-genitive. In which sentence could you also use an 's'-genitive?

1. The door/room opened but nobody was there.
2. The beginning/play is like this: 'If music be the food of love, play on.'
3. Did the hands/clock show midnight?
4. Is the end/world near?
5. Can you walk to the third floor/building?
6. Please sign at the top/every page.

IV. Join the two columns together.

1. a jar of	a. milk
2. a loaf of	b. soap
3. a pint of	c. toast
4. a bar of	d. honey
5. a slice of	e. bread

6 Personalpronomen (Personal pronouns)

Pronomen (Fürwörter) sind Wörter, die für andere Bezeichnungen stehen; z. B. ersetzen die **Personalpronomen** 'he' und 'she' 'Harry' bzw. 'Sally'.

Subjekt	Objekt (direkt	und indirekt)
I	*me*	*to me*
you	*you*	*to you*
he, she, it	*him, her, it*	*to him, her, it*
we	*us*	*to us*
you	*you*	*to you*
they	*them*	*to them*

- Die Unterscheidung zwischen **‚du' und ‚Sie'** existiert im Englischen nicht: Beides heißt **'you'** (klein geschrieben, außer am Satzanfang).

- **‚Man'** wird im Englischen meist durch **'you'** ausgedrückt, z. B.

  You can get a nice cup of coffee here.

- Nur bei **Menschen** und **(benannten) Haustieren** unterscheidet man bei Personalpronomen das Geschlecht (**'he'** oder **'she'**). Bei **Sachen** steht **'it',** z. B.

  What's Lynn's age? – She's 15.
  My dog's name? – He's called Floppy.
  Is that dog black? – Yes, it is.
  Is this your watch? – Yes, it is.

- **Nach 'to be'** bevorzugt man, anders als im Deutschen, die **Objektform,** z. B.

  Who is it? – It's me. Mark.

- Das Pronomen **'they'** wird oft verwendet, wenn man über eine **Gruppe oder eine Einzelperson,** die man nicht kennt, spricht, z. B.

  I've spoken to the teachers and they are all coming.
  If anybody rings, tell them I'll call back later.

- Vorsicht: **'it is'** und **'it has'** heißen beide, abgekürzt, **'it's',** z. B.

  It's a glorious day, isn't it?
  It's been a lovely party, hasn't it?

6 Exercises

I. Read each mini-dialogue and add an appropriate personal pronoun to the second line. ●●

1. Do you think I can get the job?
   Well, it depends on …, I suppose.
2. Are you in favour of smoking in public?
   To be honest, I'm against … .
3. What do you think of my new trousers?
   Mmm. I really like … .
4. Is my hair a bit too long?
   No, … is fine, I think.
5. What shall I do with this food?
   Give it to … . I'll eat it!
6. Who used the milk last?
   I don't know but it wasn't …!
7. I'm surprised Tracy married Kevin.
   She must love … .
8. Did Steve pass the test?
   No, … didn't.

II. Use the expressions in the box to complete the sentences. ●●

difficult • important • lovely • necessary • right • use

1. Is it … in your opinion to have two cars when the roads are so busy?
2. Come in! It's … to see you again! How are you?
3. Never mind. It's no … crying over spilt (*verdorbene*) milk!
4. Is it really … to get to the airport two hours before departure?
5. Some people think it's … to be able to operate a computer.
6. She speaks so quickly. It's … to understand what she says, isn't it?

III. What does the ''s' after the 'it' mean? – 'is' or 'has'?

1. It's raining.
2. It's had enough.
3. It's sad.
4. It's no use complaining.

IV. Who is the 'they' referring to in these sentences? Have a guess!

1. They want to put up the tax on petrol.
2. They wanted to have a Channel Tunnel over 100 years ago.
3. They don't make these shoes in half sizes. I'm very sorry.
4. They say *Short and Sharp* is a marvellous film. Have you seen it yet?

7 Possessivpronomen (Possessive pronouns)
Reflexivpronomen (Reflexive pronouns)
Pronomen der Gegenseitigkeit (Reciprocal pronouns)

- Das **Possessivpronomen** bildet zwei Formen: die adjektivische, die ein Substantiv näher beschreibt ('my car'), und die substantivische, die anstelle eines Substantivs steht ('Is it your car? – Yes, it's mine (= my car).').

adjektivisch		**substantivisch**	
my	mein(e)	***mine***	meine(s)
your	dein(e)	***yours***	deine(s)
his, her, its	sein(e), ihr(e), sein(e)	***his, hers, its***	seine(s), ihre(s), seine(s)
our	unser(e)	***ours***	unsere(s)
your	euer(e)/Ihr(e)	***yours***	eure(s)/Ihre(s)
their	ihr(e)	***theirs***	ihre(s)

Die englischen Possessivpronomen sind **nicht von Geschlecht oder Zahl** des zugehörigen Substantivs **abhängig.**

Vorsicht: **'their'** und das Adverb **'there'** sind lautlich identisch: /ðeə/.

- Die Formen des **Reflexivpronomens 'oneself'** (*sich*) benützt man, wenn Subjekt und Objekt identisch sind.

myself	***yourself***	***himself, herself, itself***
ourselves	***yourselves***	***themselves***

Die englischen Reflexivpronomen entsprechen auch dem deutschen **‚selbst'**, z. B.

Did they really do it themselves?

Eine große Zahl im Deutschen reflexiver Verben bleibt im Englischen **ohne Reflexivpronomen,** z. B.

to apologize	(**s.** entschuldigen)	***to look forward to***	(**s.** freuen auf)
to remember	(**s.** erinnern)	***to thank sb***	(**s.** bei jmdm. bedanken)
to imagine	(**s.** vorstellen)	***to be late***	(**s.** verspäten)

- Das **Pronomen der Gegenseitigkeit:** Kann man im Deutschen dem Reflexivpronomen **‚sich'** sinnvoll **‚gegenseitig'** hinzufügen, verwendet man im Englischen die Formen **'each other'** oder **'one another',** z. B.

They don't like each other. *They often argue with one another.*

7 Exercises

I. Complete the mini-dialogues using possessive pronouns.

1. My feet hurt!
   So do …!
2. I've got your jacket, haven't I?
   Yes, that's right. So where's …?
3. My wife's left her handbag somewhere.
   Is this …?
4. This isn't his house, is it?
   No. … is not so big.
5. Our parents always complain about the loud music.
   … do, too!

II. Complete these mini-dialogues using the correct form of 'oneself'.

1. May I introduce …? My name's John.
   Hello. I'm Jeremy. Jeremy Paxton.
2. We're back!
   So soon! Didn't you enjoy …?
3. Thanks for the invitation.
   Not at all. Come in. And help … to some food.
4. Is this knife sharp?
   Yes, very. Don't hurt …!
5. Bye, Steve.
   Bye, Tanya. Take care of … .

III. Decide between a form of 'oneself' or 'each other' to complete these mini-dialogues. ●●

1. I'm sure we'll get on well with … .
   Yes, I'm sure we will.
2. Did the girls hurt … seriously in the accident?
   No, they didn't.
3. Don't you recognize … in the photo?
   No! Is that really me!
4. Are they having problems with …?
   Yes, I'm afraid they are.
5. We're all new here, aren't we?
   Yes. Perhaps we should introduce … to … .

8 Fragepronomen (Interrogative pronouns)
Demonstrativpronomen (Demonstrative pronouns)

- Die **Fragepronomen** bei **Personen** lauten:

who?	(wer?)	*Who paid?*
who?	(wen?; seltener: ***whom?***)	*Who(m) did you ask?*
whose?	(wessen?)	*Whose coat is this?*
who(m) ... to/from?	(zu/von wem?)	*Who(m) did you talk to?*

Die Fragepronomen bei **Sachen** lauten:

what?	(was? – im Allgemeinen)	*What are you wearing to the party?*
which?	(welche? – aus einer Anzahl)	*Which colour do you like best?*

Präpositionen, die in Verbindung mit einem Fragepronomen stehen, verbleiben **bei dem zugehörigen Verb,** z. B.

Who were you laughing at?
What are you looking for?

- Es gibt vier **Demonstrativpronomen:**

	Einzahl	**Mehrzahl**
etwas Näherliegendes	***this*** →***x***	***these*** →***xxx***
etwas Fernliegendes	***that*** → ***x***	***those*** → ***xxx***

Mit Demonstrativpronomen kann man die **Aufmerksamkeit** des Zuhörenden gezielt **lenken.** Die Pronomen 'this' und 'these' beziehen sich auf Sachen und Personen, die nahe des Sprechenden liegen, die Pronomen 'that' und 'those' auf Dinge und Personen, die vom Sprechenden entfernt liegen (**im räumlichen, zeitlichen oder geistigen Sinn**), z. B.

This car (here) is mine.
Do you remember that day we went skiing together?
I don't like that song.

8 Exercises

I. Join the two columns together to form natural pairs.

1. why?	a. my brother's
2. who?	b. nothing
3. what?	c. tomorrow
4. when?	d. because
5. whose?	e. we

II. Which questions will provide you with the missing information?

1. The train arrived at .?. .
2. He didn't come to the meeting because .?. .
3. .?. phoned me last night.
4. Jenny saw .?. yesterday afternoon.
5. It was .?.'s mistake, not ours!

III. Translate these questions into English making sure the preposition is at the end.

1. Von wem ist das Geschenk?
2. Worüber müssen wir schreiben?
3. Woher kommen Sie?
4. Für wen ist dieser Brief?
5. Auf welchen Stuhl kann ich mich setzen?

IV. Put in 'this', 'that', 'these' or 'those' to complete these sentences. ●●

1. Come here! Look at … pictures in the paper!
2. What was … film about you saw last week?
3. You look different. Are … new glasses?
4. Mmm. … melon tastes delicious!
5. Where are … letters I forgot to take with me?
6. What was … ? I couldn't hear you.

9 Relativpronomen (Relative pronouns)

Relativpronomen leiten **bestimmende** (d.h. zum Verständnis notwendige; ohne Kommas im Englischen) und **nicht bestimmende Relativsätze** (nicht notwendige; mit Kommas) ein (s. unit 46), z.B.

The people who live next door to us are from Australia.
Mr Sinclair, who worked in our company for ten years, has got a new job.

Zu den wichtigsten Relativpronomen im Englischen gehören **'who', 'whose', 'which', 'that'** und **'where':**

- Die Relativpronomen **'who'** und **'whose'** beziehen sich auf **Personen,** wobei 'who' Subjekt wie Objekt des Relativsatzes sein kann, z.B.

  The man who works here is a friend of mine.
  The boy (who) we saw in the bus goes to our school.
  Tim, whose father was a footballer, doesn't like sport himself.

- Die Relativpronomen **'which'** und **'whose'** beziehen sich auf **Sachen.** Das Pronomen 'which' kann Subjekt wie Objekt des Relativsatzes sein, z.B.

  The train which is late is coming from Scotland.
  The money (which) they found on the street was not worth anything.
  I once knew a girl whose hair was green.

- Die Objektform **'whom'** gehört weitgehend der formalen Schriftsprache an.

- Sind **'who'** und **'which' Objekt eines bestimmenden Relativsatzes,** werden sie, v.a. in der gesprochenen Sprache, **weggelassen.** Man spricht dann von 'contact clauses', z.B.

  The meal you made last night was lovely.

- Das Relativpronomen **'that'** bezieht sich auf **Personen** und **Sachen,** aber nur in **bestimmenden Relativsätzen,** z.B.

  The dog that just walked past us sometimes bites.
  The accident (that) we saw yesterday was shown on TV.

- Das Relativpronomen **'where'** bezieht sich auf einen **Ort,** z.B.

  This is the shop where you can get the best service.

9 Exercises

I. Put in 'who' or 'which' to complete these sentences. ●●

1. What's the name of the man ... rang this morning?
2. The plane, ... was carrying over 300 passengers, crashed over Scotland.
3. I never found out the name of the person ... lent me the money.
4. This is the article in the paper ... caused all the problems.
5. The hurricane, ... came in the middle of the night, destroyed the whole house.
6. My sister, ... lives in South Africa, has not been home for ten years.

In how many sentences can you use 'that' instead of 'who' or 'which'? Two, three or five?

II. Add 'whose' or 'where' to complete these sentences.
(In one sentence you need 'who'!)

1. Have you been back to the place ... you were born?
2. We once met a man ... father was a millionaire.
3. If you don't like it, take it back to the shop ... you bought it.
4. What's the name of the girl ... has a brother in your football team?
5. The campsite ... we stayed wasn't too clean.
6. I'd like to live in a country ... it's not so cold.

III. Which relative pronoun is the object of the relative clause and can be left out?

1. Have you found the money which you lost?
2. The flight which we booked was more expensive than yours.
3. The jacket which she bought is too small for her.
4. Is that the man who shouted at you?
5. Tracy is the only person who really understands me.
6. Have you read the story *The Man that Disappeared*?

IV. Read this extract from a novel. ●●

Our summers there were easily the best things of my early childhood. Pine forests and hot sun, red deer (*Rotwild*), black and red squirrels (*Eichhörnchen*), acres of blueberries and wild strawberries; nine or ten different kinds of edible (*genießbaren*) mushrooms which we went into the forest to pick.

(From *Goodbye to All That* by Robert Graves)

10 Mengenbezeichnungen (Quantifiers)

Zu den wichtigsten **Mengenbezeichnungen** gehören:

some	einige, manche, etwas (in positiven Aussagen), z.B. *He bought some coffee.* etwas (oder unübersetzt; in Fragen, v.a. wenn man um etwas bittet), z.B. *Could I have some more tea, please?*
any	einige, manche, irgendetwas (in Fragen und Verneinungen), z.B. *Can you speak any foreign languages?*
much	viel (bei nicht zählbaren Begriffen in Fragen und Verneinungen), z.B. *They haven't got much time.*
many	viele (bei zählbaren Begriffen in Fragen und Verneinungen), z.B. *How many people live in Germany?*
a lot of/ lots of	viel(e) (bei zählbaren und nicht zählbaren Begriffen in Aussagesätzen), z.B. *He's got a lot of/lots of friends.*
a little	etwas, ein wenig (nur bei nicht zählbaren Begriffen), z.B. *We've got little experience in that field.*
a few	einige, ein paar (nur bei zählbaren Begriffen), z.B. *There are still a few days until Christmas.*
several	einige (nur bei zählbaren Begriffen), z.B. *There are several ways of getting to Britain.*
every	jede/r/s (allgemein), z.B. *They go swimming every Sunday morning.*
each	jede/r/s (einzelne), z.B. *Each student has to do the exam.*

Es gibt eine Reihe von **Wortzusammensetzungen** ('compounds') mit **'some'** und **'any'**, z.B.

someone	***somebody***	***something***	***somewhere***
anyone	***anybody***	***anything***	***anywhere***

10 Exercises

I. Complete these sentences with 'some' or 'any' or their compounds. ●●

1. There's … at the door. Can you answer it?
2. I said hello but he didn't say … back to me.
3. I like … English beer, but not all.
4. I haven't read … of the books you lent me. I've had no time.
5. Did you take … photos at the party?
6. I'd like … information about trains to Edinburgh, please.
7. I'm not having … to eat today. I'm on a diet.
8. Has … seen Kevin this morning?

II. Put in 'much', 'many' or 'a lot of' to complete these sentences.

1. There wasn't … milk in the fridge so I bought you some more.
2. How … hours is the flight from Berlin to New York?
3. We had … snow last winter, didn't we?
4. I haven't got … time but I'll try and help you.
5. Would you like some more wine? – Yes, please, but not too … .
6. We've got … friends but we don't have … time to see them.
7. … people prefer to work for themselves nowadays.
8. Do you know if there are … tickets left for next Saturday's match?

III. Is it 'a few' or 'a little'? Complete the sentences using the correct form.

1. We last saw Jackie … weeks ago.
2. They only had … English money with them.
3. He can speak … words of German.
4. More steak and kidney pie? – Yes, please, but only … .

IV. Identify the correct word in the brackets to complete the sentence.

1. We go jogging (each/several/every) Tuesday and Thursday.
2. She had four children and (many/each/any) of them have had four children, too.
3. (Many/Every/All) people in our company speak English fluently.
4. There are (all/several/each) shops in town where you can hire skis.

11 Adjektive (Adjectives)

Das Adjektiv besitzt **zwei Steigerungsformen,** um Personen, Dinge und Ereignisse miteinander vergleichen zu können. Diese Formen nennt man **Komparativ** und **Superlativ:**

- **Einsilbige Adjektive** werden durch **Anhängen von -er, -est** gesteigert; ein einzelner Endkonsonant wird nach kurzem Vokal verdoppelt, z. B.

  long → longer → the longest *big → bigger → the biggest*

- **Drei- und mehrsilbige Adjektive** steigert man durch **'more', 'most',** z. B.

  difficult → more difficult → the most difficult
  excited → more excited → the most excited

- **Zweisilbige Adjektive** werden mit **-er, -est** *oder* **'more', 'most'** gesteigert:

  Adjektive, die auf **-er, -le, -y** und **-ow** enden, hängen i. d. R. **-er, -est** an, z. B.

  simple → simpler → the simplest
  narrow → narrower → the narrowest

  Die **übrigen** zweisilbigen Adjektive steigert man mit **'more', 'most'**, z. B.

  helpful → more helpful → the most helpful
  nervous → more nervous → the most nervous

- **Sonderformen:**

bad	→	***worse***	→	***the worst***
good	→	***better***	→	***the best***
much	→	***more***	→	***the most***
little	→	***less***	→	***the least***

- Die englische Konstruktion **'the' + Komparativ + 'the' + Komparativ** entspricht dem deutschen **‚je … desto'**, z. B.

  The longer we wait, the more nervous I get.

- Die englische Konstruktion **'get'/'become' + Komparativ + Komparativ** entspricht dem deutschen **‚werden' + ‚immer' + Komparativ,** z. B.

  Your English is getting better and better.

11 Exercises

I. Use a comparative form of the words in the box to complete these sentences. ●●

busy • easy • expensive • good • happy • important • quiet • serious • thin

1. Gosh! You've lost a lot of weight, haven't you? You look much …!
2. What is … for you? An interesting job or a well-paid job?
3. His illness was … than the doctors first thought.
4. Don't you think everyone seems … now that summer is here?
5. Are the … hotels in the centre of the city or on the outskirts?
6. He used to talk all the time but recently he's become … .
7. The town seems … today. Is anything special happening?
8. The test was … than I expected and I did … in the end.

II. Complete the sentences below using a superlative form of the adjective in brackets. ●●

1. Which is the … (good) holiday you've ever had?
2. She is one of the … (intelligent) people I've worked with.
3. It was the … (embarrassing) situation you could imagine.
4. I think you could say it was the … (happy) day of my life.
5. It's one of the … (demanding) jobs that you can possibly do.

III. Form five meaningful sentences by linking the half-sentences.

1. The more I got to know her
2. The earlier you start
3. The harder you work
4. The hotter the weather
5. The more expensive the hotel

a. the more difficult it becomes.
b. the more tired I feel.
c. the more money you can earn.
d. the larger the rooms.
e. the sooner you'll finish.
f. the more I liked her.
g. the more generous they were.

IV. Translate these sentences into English. Use the verb 'get'.

1. Die Warteschlange (*queue*) wird immer länger.
2. Essen gehen (*eating out*) wird immer teurer.
3. Das Leben wird immer komplizierter.
4. Die Welt wird immer kleiner.

12 Adverbien (Adverbs)

Es gibt **Adverbien** des **Ortes** ('at home'), der **Zeit** ('in a minute'), der **Häufigkeit** ('rarely'), des **Grades** ('quite') und der **Art und Weise** ('carefully').
Viele Adverbien können als Vokabeln gelernt werden ('in a minute' = gleich).

Die **Adverbien der Art und Weise** werden **von Adjektiven abgeleitet:**

- Die meisten Adverbien der Art und Weise werden durch **Anhängen von -ly** gebildet. Sie **bestimmen** ein Verb, Adjektiv oder weiteres Adverb **näher,** z. B.

  Please drive carefully. (Das Adverb beschreibt das Verb 'drive'.)
  She is particularly shy. (Das Adverb beschreibt das Adjektiv 'shy'.)
  He behaved extremely badly. (Das Adverb beschreibt das Adverb 'badly'.)

  Besonderheiten:

happy	→	*happily*	(-y wird zu -i)
nice	→	*nicely*	(Schluss-e bleibt)
simple	→	*simply*	(-le wird zu -ly)
automatic	→	*automatically*	(-ic wird zu -ically)

- Einige **Adjektive und Adverbien,** wie 'fast' und 'hard', sind **identisch,** z. B.

  It's a fast car. (Adjektiv) *She drives fast.* (Adverb)

- Ausnahme: **'good'** (Adjektiv) → **'well'** (Adverb)

  We speak very good English. *We speak English very well.*

- Es gibt einige **Adjektive,** die **auf -ly** enden. Das zugehörige **Adverb** muss deshalb **anders gebildet** werden, z. B.

  A silly smile. (Adjektiv) *He behaved in a silly way.* (Adverb)

- Vorsicht bei **hardly:** Die deutsche Entsprechung heißt **‚kaum'**, z. B.

  I hardly recognized you.

- Bei **Verben,** die **keine echte Handlung** ausdrücken (s. unit 33), steht **kein Adverb,** sondern ein Adjektiv, z. B.

  You look beautiful! *The wine tastes sour.*
  The food smells delicious. *Your idea sounds good.*

12 Exercises

I. Complete the sentences by using the words in brackets as adverbs.

1. His brother is (constant) complaining about him.
2. Did success come (easy)?
3. She can dance (brilliant).
4. They work (hard) because they have to.
5. The press reacted (positive).
6. Do you see each other (regular)?
7. She's only three years old but she speaks (extreme) (good), doesn't she?
8. They behaved (bad) and were asked to leave the room (immediate).

II. Adjective or adverb? Identify the correct word in the brackets. ●●

1. Could you please come in (quiet/quietly). The baby's sleeping very (light/lightly).
2. The crowd clapped (loud/loudly) and (enthusiastic/enthusiastically).
3. She seemed (angry/angrily) on the phone. What was the matter (exact/exactly)?
4. Your parents visit you quite (frequent/frequently) so I suppose they live (local/locally).
5. He was (bitter/bitterly) disappointed not to win a prize.
6. You speak English very (good/well). How did you learn to speak it so (fluent/fluently)?
7. The food tastes (excellent/excellently)! Congratulations.
8. You're always so (slow/slowly)! Can't you do things more (quick/quickly)?

III. Complete this short text. Use the correct form of the word in brackets. ●●

There's been a small argument in the Pollingworth family. Jane, 17, has complained that Michael, 21, plays his music too (loud). She says that she can (hard) do her homework. Mike sees things (different). He says he needs background music to concentrate (proper) on his studies. He's working very (hard) for his final exams in the summer. Mr Pollingworth takes his children's problem (serious). 'We'll have to find a solution (immediate),' he says. 'I know. I'll buy Michael some headphones.' Mike is (real) pleased with his father's suggestion but Jane seems less (happy). 'That's not very (nice),' she thinks. 'Why can't I have some headphones, too?'

13 Präpositionen und Konjunktionen (Prepositions and conjunctions)

Präpositionen (Verhältniswörter) stehen **vor** einem **Substantiv, Pronomen** oder **Gerund,** z.B.

We went by bus.
I talked to them.
We are interested in having a holiday in Ireland.

- Viele Präpositionen lernt man am besten im **Kontext,** z.B.

Can I pay by cheque?	(mit Scheck)
I'm sorry. I did it by mistake.	(aus Versehen)
I'd like to sit by the window.	(neben dem Fenster)

- Präpositionen können am **Ende eines Satzes** vorkommen, v.a. bei Fragen, z.B.

What are you afraid of? *Who were you talking about?*

Konjunktionen (Bindewörter) **verbinden Satzteile** und **leiten Haupt- und Nebensätze ein,** z.B.

She felt ill, but she went to work.
Although she lives in Germany, she can't speak German.

- **Wichtige Konjunktionen:**

after	*We left after we had paid the bill.*	(nachdem)
although	*We decided to buy it although it was expensive.*	(obwohl)
as	*He hurt himself as he was getting off his bike.*	(während)
because	*We can't come because we haven't got the time.*	(weil)
before	*Let's go before it gets too busy.*	(bevor, ehe)
but	*I can't dance but I like to watch them dancing.*	(aber)
if	*You can start work later if you wish.*	(wenn, falls)
in order to	*We've come in order to help you.*	(um … zu)
since	*Have you been happy since you changed your job?*	(seit(dem))
so that	*She took the train so that she could do some work.*	(damit)
unless	*Nobody will tell you what to do unless you ask.*	(wenn … nicht)
until	*We'll wait until you give us a signal.*	(bis)
when	*Could you ring us when you get home?*	(wenn, als)
whether	*I'm not sure whether I am the right person to help.*	(ob)
while	*While you're waiting you can do the washing-up!*	(während)

13 Exercises

I. Complete the sentences by using a preposition of time: 'at', 'on' or 'in'.

1. Will you be … home tonight?
2. The meeting begins … October 17, … 9 o'clock.
3. Can I phone you … Tuesday morning?
4. Hurry up, will you! We're going … two minutes.
5. What are you doing … New Year's Eve?
6. I'm just going out. I'll be back … half an hour.

II. Underline the correct preposition of place in the brackets. ●●

1. Do you take sugar (with, on, at) your tea?
2. The post office is 100 metres from here (at, on, by) the left.
3. Would you like to live (on, at, in) the country?
4. Did you see the robin (*Rotkehlchen*) (at, with, on) that fence?
5. I'll write my name and address (in, on, at) the back of this piece of paper.
6. Have you ever been (in, to, from) Wales?
7. Her parents live (to, by, in) the middle of Birmingham, I believe.
8. Were you (in, on, at) the cinema last night?

III. These are everyday expressions. Which prepositions are missing? ●●

1. No cake for me. I'm … a diet!
2. Shall we go … a walk?
3. Have you read any books … Nick Hornby?
4. Did you see that programme … TV last night?
5. I'm not very good … telling jokes.
6. You're not frightened … dogs, are you?

IV. Which conjunction is needed to complete the following sentences? ●●

1. We'll stay here … you get back.
2. … we had to get up early the next day, we decided to watch the late-night film.
3. I've stopped eating butter … lose some weight.
4. We can't go on holiday this year … we can't afford it.
5. Have you seen any of your schoolfriends … you left school?
6. … you go, you must give me your phone number, please.
7. I'm not coming with you, … you like it or not.
8. Unfortunately we got to the station … the train had left.

14 Primäre Hilfsverben (Primary auxiliaries)

'be', 'do' und **'have'** spielen eine zentrale Rolle in der englischen Grammatik.

- Mit dem **Hilfsverb 'be'** kann man alle **Verlaufsformen** (s. units 26, 28, 30, 32 u. 34f.) und **Passivformen** (s. unit 38) bilden, z. B.

  She is having a bath at the moment.
  He has been working as a painter for ten years.
  We were given your number.

- Mit dem **Hilfsverb 'do'** kann man **Fragen, Verneinungen, Kurzformen** und **Befehlsformen** bilden, z. B.

  Do you live here? *Does she smoke? – No, she doesn't.*
  We did not see you. *Don't ask me! Ask them!*

- Mit dem **Hilfsverb 'have'** kann man die zusammengesetzten Zeiten **Present Perfect, Past Perfect** und **Future Perfect** bilden (s. units 29, 31 u. 35), z. B.

  We have driven here.
  The bus had already gone.
  Computers will have become more powerful by next year.

- Die **Kurzformen (Hilfsverb + 'not')** sind in der gesprochenen Sprache sehr gebräuchlich, z. B.

isn't	*hasn't*	*doesn't*	*wasn't*	*hadn't*
aren't	*haven't*	*don't*	*weren't*	*didn't*

- Das Verb **'be'** wird auch als **Vollverb** verwendet. Fragen bildet man durch Umstellen. Zur Verneinung benötigt man 'not'. 'be' kommt oft in Verbindung mit **'there'** vor: Es drückt aus, dass etwas vorhanden ist, z. B.

  Have you heard? There's going to be snow tomorrow.

- Auch die Verben **'do'** und **'have'** sind **Vollverben.** Für Fragen und Verneinungen in der einfachen Gegenwart und einfachen Vergangenheit benötigt man zusätzlich 'do', 'does' und 'did' (s. unit 23), z. B.

  What do you do? *Does she do her work well?*
  Do you have any brothers or sisters? *When did you have breakfast?*

14 Exercises

I. Read through the sentences and decide if the word underlined is a full verb or an auxiliary.

1. What do you do?
2. We didn't know you liked jazz.
3. Are you doing anything this evening?
4. Do you do any sport?
5. Did you want to ask me something?
6. We haven't done our homework.
7. She's been doing the course for six months.
8. Didn't you realize it was me?

Full verb	Auxiliary

II. Only one of the following sentences does not contain a passive form of the verb. Can you find it?

1. I am being picked up at seven.
2. Has the meal been paid for?
3. English is spoken all over the world.
4. When are you leaving for your holiday?
5. Were you given this as a present?

III. Which two of the following questions contain a perfect form (present perfect, past perfect or future perfect)?

1. How long have you been in this country?
2. Have you got any small change?
3. Are you having a cup of tea with us?
4. My letter will have reached you by the weekend.
5. To be quite honest we don't really have the time to go out at the weekend.

IV. How many of the following verbs are in the continuous form?

1. Do you live near here?
2. Have you ever worked abroad?
3. I am looking for a book by David Lodge.
4. You will be met at the airport.

15 Modale Hilfsverben I (Modal auxiliaries I)

can could may might will would shall should must

- Modale Hilfsverben sind **‚unvollständig'**, weil sie nur ***eine* Zeitform, keinen Infinitiv** und **kein Partizip** aufweisen und die **dritte Person Einzahl ohne -s** bilden, z. B.

  He may come later.

- Sie können nur in **Verbindung mit einem Vollverb** verwendet werden, z. B.

  I'll see you soon.

- Die **Frageform** eines Hilfsverbs wird durch **Umstellen** von Subjekt und Hilfsverb gebildet; zur **Verneinung** verwendet man **'not'**, z. B.

  Must you say that? *They may not have time.*

- Modale Hilfsverben können **Vergangenes, Gegenwärtiges** oder **Zukünftiges** beschreiben, z. B.

  I could ride a bike when I was three. (Vergangenheit)
  Could you help me do this exercise? (Gegenwart)
  We could go away next weekend. (Zukunft)

- Modale Hilfsverben können auch **mit 'have' und dem Partizip Perfekt kombiniert** werden (s. unit 19), z. B.

  You could have told me. *She must have known.*
  We should have warned you. *I would have helped you.*

- Mit modalen Hilfsverben wird der Aussage des Vollverbs eine weitere Bedeutung hinzugefügt: Modale (Modus = Art und Weise) Hilfsverben sagen, was möglich, wahrscheinlich, notwendig etc. ist. Ein modales Hilfsverb kann also eine Reihe von **Sprechabsichten** ausdrücken, z. B.

  She can run a marathon in under three hours. (Fähigkeit)
  Can I ring you later? (Bitte)
  I can get you a beer if you want. (Angebot)
  I can come to the party but I don't really want to. (Möglichkeit)
  We can go to the cinema, can't we? (Vorschlag)

15 Exercises

I. Which of the following sentences expresses a fact and which expresses the speaker's opinion?

1. His son is very tall.
2. His son must be very tall.

II. Which of the following sentences expresses a fact and which expresses the speaker's feeling?

1. She may be at home.
2. She is at home.

*III. Which of the following sentences expresses a fact and which expresses the speaker's attitude (*Einstellung*)?*

1. People shouldn't do things like that.
2. People don't do things like that.

IV. Which of the following questions asks for a fact and which asks for the listener's judgement?

1. Did you leave them in your office?
2. Could you have left them in your office?

V. Which function is expressed by the modal auxiliary in each sentence? Choose your answer from the box below. ●●

deduction (*Schlussfolgerung*) • invitation • offer • permission • possibility refusal • request • suggestion

1. Could you pass the salt, please?
2. Of course you may borrow our ladder!
3. We might go to Scotland for a few days.
4. Can we give you a lift home?
5. She won't tell us where she's going.
6. Shall we go for a walk after lunch?
7. Would you like to come with us?
8. He must be over 60, don't you think?

16 Modale Hilfsverben II (Modal auxiliaries II)

- Mit den modalen Hilfsverben **'can'/'can't'/'could'/'couldn't'** verbinden wir u. a. folgende **Sprechabsichten:**

I can do it.	(Fähigkeit)
I can't help you.	(Unfähigkeit)
You can borrow my car.	(Erlaubnis)
You can't be serious!	(Unmöglichkeit)
You can't use my PC.	(Verbot)
Could we have the answers?	(Bitte)
Couldn't we stay at home?	(Vorschlag)

- Mit den modalen Hilfsverben **'may'/'may not'/'might'/'mightn't'** verbinden wir u. a. folgende **Sprechabsichten:**

May I come in for a second?	(Bitte)
You may smoke in this room.	(Erlaubnis)
That mightn't be a bad idea.	(Möglichkeit)
He may have been here.	(Schlussfolgerung)

- Mit dem modalen Hilfsverb **'must'** bzw. **'mustn't'** verbinden wir u. a. folgende **Sprechabsichten:**

I really must go now.	(Notwendigkeit)
You must show your tickets here.	(Zwang)
She must have forgotten to ring.	(Schlussfolgerung)
He really must go to the doctor.	(Rat)

Vorsicht: Die Konstruktion **'mustn't'** entspricht dem deutschen **‚nicht dürfen'** (s. unit 18), z. B.

You mustn't park here.	(Verbot)

16 Exercises

I. Use 'can' or 'could' to form questions. You want to ask someone if he or she …

1. … knows how to use a computer.
2. … is willing to lend you some money.
3. … knows how to speak French.
4. … needs help with his or her homework.
5. … is able to play a musical instrument.
6. … needs something to drink.
7. … has finished with the dictionary you need.
8. … is in a position to give you some advice.

II. In which of the following sentences does 'may' express permission?

1. He may come with us. He needs to ask his wife first.
2. May I open the window? It's very warm in here.
3. It may snow later this week.
4. May I borrow your car for a day?
5. It may be too late.
6. May I ring after nine?

III. Rewrite the following sentences using 'might'.

1. Perhaps he is at home.
2. Maybe it'll rain later.
3. Perhaps we will go to England in the summer.
4. Maybe she'll have time.
5. Perhaps they'll give us a lift to the airport.
6. Maybe we'll move house next year.

IV. Add 'must' or 'mustn't' to the following sentences.

1. You … remember to pay.
2. You … forget to pay.
3. We … fly back home without buying some English tea.
4. We … buy some English tea before we fly back home.
5. If I come to the party, I … leave by midnight.
6. If I come to the party, I … stay later than midnight.

17 Modale Hilfsverben III (Modal auxiliaries III)

- Die Hilfsverben **'will'/'won't'/'would'/'wouldn't'** bringen zum Ausdruck, z. B.

Will you have another piece of cake?	(Angebot)
You will do exactly what I've said.	(Befehl)
I'll see you later.	(Versprechen)
I'll have a cheese roll, please.	(Bitte)
Would you like to come round and visit us?	(Angebot)
If you say that again, I'll get very angry.	(Drohung)
No, I won't do it. I'm sorry.	(Weigerung)

Eine **Form der Zukunft** im Englischen und **Hilfsverb** zugleich ist **'will'** (s. unit 34). 'will' bringt die Meinung des Sprechenden zum Zeitpunkt des Sprechens zum Ausdruck. Im Deutschen stehen solche Äußerungen, meist spontane Reaktionen auf bestimmte Situationen, häufig in der Gegenwartsform, z. B.

I'll call you later.	(Ich rufe dich später an.)
I'll have a cup of tea, please.	(Ich nehme eine Tasse Tee, bitte.)

Vorsicht: **'want'** und **'won't'** (= 'will not') werden unterschiedlich ausgesprochen, z. B.

We won't see you next week.	/wəʊnt/
We want to go away.	/wɒnt/

Vorsicht: Das deutsche **,will nicht'** heißt **'don't want to'** im Englischen, z. B.

I don't want to play.	(Ich will nicht spielen.)

Das Hilfsverb **'would'** ist sehr gebräuchlich. Mit 'would' kann man **höflich fragen** oder in einem Geschäftsbrief um etw. **bitten,** z. B.

Would you like something to eat?
I would be grateful if you could send us your latest catalogue.

- Die Hilfsverben **'shall'** und **'should'** sind weniger gebräuchlich, z. B.

Shall I help you?	(Angebot)
Shall we go out for a drink?	(Vorschlag)
You should really tell him what happened.	(Rat)
I should have gone to the meeting.	(Verpflichtung)
They should be home soon.	(Schlussfolgerung)

17 Exercises

I. Give some advice to the people in the following situations. Begin your sentences with 'I think you should …'. ●●

1. Your friend has got bad toothache.
2. Your friend is going to California and he/she can't speak English.
3. Your friend is bored with the job he/she does.
4. Your friend smokes 80 cigarettes a day.

II. Locate the most appropriate response (a–d) to the following sentences (1–4). ●●

1. Would you like some tea?
2. Would you come this way, please.
3. Would you like us to meet you at home?
4. Would you take a seat, please.

a. Thank you very much.
b. Oh, that would be lovely.
c. No, thank you. I've just had a cup.
d. Yes, certainly.

III. Find the appropriate response or comment (a–h) in the following situations (1–6). (Be careful, there are more responses than situations!) ●●

1. The door keeps banging because the window is open.
2. You are going out for the evening.
3. You are leaving for a three-week holiday.
4. You are in a restaurant and talking to the waiter.
5. Somebody's invited you to have dinner with them.
6. A friend of yours forgot to buy some milk.

a. I'll catch it.
b. I'll have the soup.
c. I'll do the washing-up.
d. I'll close it.
e. I'll get some for you.
f. I'll see you later.
g. I'll fax you the answer.
h. I'll send you a postcard.

18 Modale Hilfsverben IV (Modal auxiliaries IV)

- Das **Modalverb 'must'** drückt , wie alle Modalverben, die Meinung des Sprechenden zum Zeitpunkt des Sprechens aus. Bei 'must' handelt es sich i.d.R. um eine **selbst auferlegte Notwendigkeit,** z.B.

  We must try and save some money.
  Must you leave now?

  'must' bezieht sich nur auf Gegenwart und Zukunft. Als **Vergangenheitsform** verwendet man die Ersatzform **'have to'** (s. unit 22), z.B.

  Did you have to walk all the way here?
  He had to take a taxi because he missed the bus.

- Das **Vollverb 'have to'** drückt eine **Notwendigkeit** aus, die nicht – wie bei 'must' – vom Sprechenden selbst, sondern **von außen auferlegt** wird, d.h. von einer anderen Person oder Situation, z.B.

  We had to wait in the queue. (Norm)
  When do we have to start work in the morning? (Tarifvertrag)

- Die **verneinten Formen** 'mustn't' und 'don't have to' haben unterschiedliche Bedeutung. Das Modalverb **'mustn't'** drückt ein **Verbot** aus; das Vollverb **'don't have to'** dagegen betont, dass **keine Notwendigkeit** besteht, etw. zu tun, z.B.

  You mustn't play football on the road. It's too dangerous.
  You don't have to hurry. We've got lots of time.

  Die Formen **'don't need to'** und **'needn't'** können **'don't have to' ersetzen,** z.B.

  You don't need to go to the shops. I can go.
  You needn't write to me if you're very busy.

Verbot	*mustn't*	nicht dürfen

nicht müssen	*don't have to/need to*	**Option**

18 Exercises

I. Link the sentences to their 'meanings'. ●●

1. I must buy some new shoes. 2. I have to buy some new shoes.	a. I feel I need some new shoes. b. People tell me I need smarter shoes.
3. You must wear a jacket. 4. You have to wear a jacket.	a. I think you need to wear a jacket. b. The restaurant manager will not let you in without a jacket.
5. I must have a drink of water. 6. I have to have a drink of water.	a. The doctor says I need to drink more. b. I'm thirsty.
7. We must buy a new car. 8. We have to buy another car.	a. We feel we need a new car. b. Our old car is too dangerous to drive.

II. Complete these mini-dialogues with 'mustn't' or 'don't'/'doesn't'/'didn't have to'. ●●

1. It's Dad's birthday next week.
   I know. I … forget to send him a card.
2. My parents didn't lend me enough money for my holiday.
   They … lend you any, did they!
3. I'm going to the shops. Shall I get you something?
   Well, you … but it'd be nice if you would!
4. I won't understand the joke.
   You … be English to understand humour like this!
5. Is it far?
   No, not at all. We … drive. We can walk, can't we?
6. Shall we take the next train?
   No, we … . It doesn't stop at the airport.

III. Two of the sentences below sound quite personal and friendly. The other sounds impersonal and much less friendly. Which sentence is it and why?

1. You must give me your address.
2. You have to give me your address.
3. You'll have to give me your address.

19 Modale Hilfsverben V (Modal auxiliaries V)

- Mit der Kombination **modales Hilfsverb + 'have' + Partizip Perfekt** lässt sich ausdrücken, was möglicherweise **geschehen sein wird, hätte können, sollen bzw. müssen.**

Everyone will have heard me.	(Jeder wird … gehört haben.)
You would have loved it in Jersey!	(Es hätte euch … gefallen!)
What can have happened to them?	(Was kann … passiert sein?)
He might have lost his passport.	(Er könnte … verloren haben.)
You might at least have asked me!	(Sie hätten … fragen können!)
We should have left the house.	(Wir hätten … verlassen sollen.)
You shouldn't have sung so loudly.	(Du hättest nicht … singen sollen.)
He must have gone home.	(Er muss … gefahren sein.)
It must have been him!	(Es muss … gewesen sein!)

- Die Kombination modales Hilfsverb + 'have' + Partizip Perfekt kann sich sowohl auf **Vergangenes als auch Zukünftiges** beziehen, z. B.

You should have used butter not margarine.
(Du hättest Butter, nicht Margarine nehmen sollen.)

One day people may have stopped eating meat.
(Eines Tages könnten die Menschen aufgehört haben, Fleisch zu essen.)

19 Exercises

I. Do these sentences describe something in the past or in the future? Mark the appropriate column.

	past	future
1. This time next year I should have finished college.		
2. You could have told us it was today!		
3. They might have warned us.		
4. One day people will have stopped using petrol in their cars.		
5. It must have been them.		
6. They would have informed us, wouldn't they?		

II. Form complete sentences using the correct forms of the words in brackets. ●●

1. She … (can, not, take) my book because it's still here.
2. She should speak more slowly. He … (may, not, understand) her.
3. They … (might, not, tell) her about the party.
4. She … (must, leave) a message with him, surely?
5. He … (should, arrive) by now, shouldn't he?
6. You … (should, not, say) that! You don't know what happened.
7. He … (might, not, go out) because his light's still on.
8. They … (must, have) a good reason to leave early.

III. Read this extract from a novel. ●●

And after all the weather was ideal. They could not have had a more perfect day for a garden party if they had ordered it. Windless, warm, the sky without a cloud. Only the blue was veiled (*verschleiert*) with haze (*Dunst*) of light gold, as it is sometimes in early summer. The gardener had been up since dawn (*Morgendämmerung*), mowing the lawns and sweeping (*fegen*) them, until the grass and the dark flat rosettes where the daisy plants (*Gänseblümchen*) had been seemed to shine. As for the roses, you could not help feeling they understood that roses are the only flowers that impress people at garden parties; the only flowers that everybody is certain of knowing.

(From *The Garden Party* by Katherine Mansfield)

20 Ersatzformen für Hilfsverben (Auxiliary substitutes)

Hilfsverben werden **‚unvollständig‘** genannt, weil sie u.a. bestimmte **Zeitformen** nicht bilden können. **Ersatzformen** für Hilfsverben, d.h. Vollverben mit ähnlicher Bedeutung, übernehmen diese Funktion.

- Das Vollverb **'to be able to' ersetzt 'can',** wenn die **Fähigkeit** zu etw., und nicht nur eine Möglichkeit, gemeint ist, z.B.

  Are you really able to drive now?
  I haven't been able to repair the bike.

- Das Vollverb **'to be (not) allowed to' ersetzt 'may', 'can't'** oder **'mustn't',** wenn es sich um eine ausdrückliche **Erlaubnis** bzw. ein zwingendes **Verbot** handelt, z.B.

  She has been allowed to go out by herself.
  You're not allowed to park here.

- Das Vollverb **'to have to' ersetzt 'must',** wenn der **Zwang,** etw. zu tun, **von außen** kommt (s. unit 18), z.B.

  We have to go. Our train leaves in five minutes.
  (aber: *We must go. We're getting very tired.*)

  Die **Vergangenheitsform** von 'to have to' und 'must' ist **'had to',** z.B.

  We're late because we had to wait so long for the bus.

  Die verneinten Formen **'don't have to'** und **'don't need to'** (s. unit 18) betonen, dass **keinerlei Notwendigkeit oder Zwang** besteht, etw. zu tun, z.B.

  You can come with us if you want but you don't have to.
  We're starting now but the others don't need to. They can start later.

  Vorsicht: Das Verb **'mustn't'** heißt **‚nicht dürfen‘** (s. unit 16); **'don't have to'/'don't need to'** dagegen **‚nicht müssen‘/‚nicht brauchen‘,** z.B.

  You mustn't say things like that!
  (So etwas darfst du nicht sagen!)
  You don't have to say things like that, do you?
  (Du musst so etwas nicht sagen, oder?)

20 Exercises

I. Add the correct form (present, present perfect, past) of the verb 'to be able to' to complete these sentences. ●●

1. My grandfather loved music. He … play the violin brilliantly.
2. They didn't have any money with them but we … lend them some.
3. I can't understand this. In fact I … (never) understand it!
4. It was very dark so they … (not) see very far.
5. She broke her leg last week so she … (not) go to work since then.

II. Use 'to be allowed to' to complete four of the following five sentences. What verb do you need in the other sentence? ●●

1. When we were children we … (not) watch much television.
2. … English children … wear what they want at school?
3. We had free tickets for the match so we … (not) pay anything.
4. … all English shops … open on Sundays?
5. The British Monarch … (not) get involved in politics.

III. Put a form of 'to have to' into these sentences. ●●

1. … you ever … go to hospital?
2. She wasn't feeling well yesterday so she … stay at home.
3. … you … to say the answer? Now everybody knows!
4. I'm leaving early tomorrow morning so I … go to bed.
5. What time … you … get up at the weekend?

IV. To complete these mini-dialogues add 'must', 'mustn't' or 'don't have to'. ●●

1. Shall I wait for you?
   No, it's alright. You … wait.
2. There's a letter here.
   Oh yes. I … forget to post it.
3. You … come and see us some time.
   Thank you. We'd love to.
4. Do you work from home?
   Yes, I do, so it means I … travel much.

21 Andere Hilfsverben (Other auxiliaries)

Es gibt eine kleine Gruppe von Verben, die in ihrer **Struktur** und **Funktion** den neun modalen Hilfsverben sehr ähnlich ist:

- Das Hilfsverb **'ought to' (+ Infinitiv)** wird wie 'should' verwendet, um einen **Rat** zu geben, z.B.

  You ought to put on a jacket. (Du solltest eine Jacke anziehen.)
  You ought to call the police. (Sie sollten die Polizei rufen.)

  Das Hilfsverb 'ought to' kann auch eine **Wahrscheinlichkeit** ausdrücken, z.B.

  It's very late so he ought to be here by now. (... dürfte er schon hier sein.)

- Das Hilfsverb **'dare'** (*wagen, sich (ge)trauen*) kommt meist in **Fragen** (als Ausruf) und **Verneinungen** vor. Der Infinitiv folgt ohne 'to', z.B.

  How dare you say such a thing!
  I dared not wake my father when he was asleep.

- Das Hilfsverb **'need'** (*brauchen, müssen*) wird wie das Vollverb 'to need to' verwendet, z.B.

  Need I come as well? (oder: *Do I need to come as well?*)
  You needn't worry. (oder: *You don't need to worry.*)

- Das Hilfsverb **'used to' (+ Infinitiv)** sagt aus, dass etw. regelmäßig in der Vergangenheit passiert ist. Diese Form wird häufig verwendet, z.B.

  We used to (/juːstə/) live on a farm.
  (Wir lebten früher auf einer Farm.)
  Did you use to read to your children?
  (Hast du früher deinen Kindern vorgelesen?)

- Auf **'would ('d) rather'** (*würde lieber*) folgt der Infinitv ohne 'to', z.B.

  I'd rather stay at home today.

- Der Ausdruck **'had ('d) better'** (*sollte besser*) steht ebenfalls immer ohne 'to', z.B.

  I'd better tell them what happened.

21 Exercises

I. Which is the correct pronunciation of the underlined words? Choose between a, b or c in the box below. ●●

a. /juːstə/	**b.** /juːz/	**c.** /juːzd/

1. She likes to use her freetime to do sport.
2. We used your car last night.
3. He used to work freelance (*freiberuflich*).
4. Did you use the CD player yesterday?
5. We didn't use to have so many divorces in this country.

II. Add 'used to' and an infinitive of your choice to complete the following sentences. ●●

1. Before they had a PC they … their letters by hand.
2. Last year we … tennis every other day but now we prefer jogging.
3. My father … cigars until recently.
4. They often … to the cinema but now they watch the films on video instead.
5. We … a TV but without it it's much better. We talk a lot more.

III. Find an appropriate reaction on the right (a–g) to the statements on the left (1–5) and form a sentence with ''d rather'. ●●

	a. (do it alone)
1. Let's eat out.	b. (walk the whole way)
2. Can you come at three?	c. (go immediately)
3. I'll give you the CD next week.	d. (have dinner at home)
4. Let's wait a bit longer.	e. (have it now)
5. Shall we take the bus?	f. (watch the match live)
	g. (come at four)

22 'have' & 'have got'

Das **Verb 'have got'** ist besonders geläufig im **britischen Englisch,** v.a. in der gesprochenen Sprache. Es hat die Bedeutung ,haben' oder ,besitzen' und wird **nicht in der Verlaufsform** verwendet:

I	***have***	***got***
you	***have***	
he, she, it	**has**	
we	***have***	
you	***have***	
they	***have***	

- **Fragen** mit 'have got' bildet man **ohne 'do'/'does'/'did'** durch Umstellen von Subjekt und Verb; zur **Verneinung** verwendet man **'not',** z.B.

  Have you got children? *She has not got time to visit us.*

- Personalpronomen und 'have got' bzw. 'have got' und 'not' werden in der gesprochenen Sprache oft **zusammengezogen,** z.B.

  She's got three brothers. *We haven't got a television.*

- In der **Vergangenheit** verwendet man nur **'had',** z.B.

  When I was small I had fair hair.

Im **amerikanischen Englisch** wird das **Vollverb 'to have'** bevorzugt (s. unit 53):

- **Fragen** und **Verneinungen** in der einfachen Gegenwart und Vergangenheit werden, wie bei allen Vollverben außer 'to be', **mit 'do'/'does'/'did'** gebildet, z.B.

  Do you have children? *She doesn't have time to visit us.*

- Wenn im **britischen Englisch** 'have' die Bedeutung **,erleben', ,essen'** oder **,trinken'** hat, wird das Vollverb 'to have' benötigt, z.B.

  We don't have English classes every week.
  When do you normally have breakfast?

- Andere **Wendungen** mit 'to have' als Vollverb:

have a party	(eine Party geben)	***have lunch***	(zu Mittag essen)
have a good time	(viel Spaß haben)	***have dinner***	(zu Abend essen)
have a bath/shower	(s. baden/duschen)	***have a drink***	(etw. trinken)
have a wash	(s. waschen)	***have fun***	(s. vergnügen)

22 Exercises

I. Form questions to ask for the correct information in the brackets. ●●

1. Daniel's got (one, two, three?) children.
2. Patricia and Malcolm have got a house in (Spain, France, Portugal?).
3. Francis has got a free evening (tomorrow, this weekend, next week?).
4. They didn't have any (milk, bread, cheese?) in the corner shop.
5. Jackie had a car in London because she (needed one, was too lazy to use the bus?).

II. What do you say to somebody in these situations? (The thing you ask for is not in the sentence!) Use an expression which begins with 'Excuse me. Have you got ... ?'. ●●

1. You don't have a watch but you need to know the ... .
2. You need to smoke and you've got a cigarette but you haven't got a ... with you.
3. You're in a car park and you need some ... for £5.
4. You need to write something but you haven't got a ... with you.
5. You want to post a letter but you haven't got a ... with you.

III. Write these British English sentences in American English.

1. Have you got a minute?
2. She's got a good job.
3. Have they got a pet?
4. We haven't got many good friends.
5. He is having lunch.

IV. Write these American English sentences in British English. ●●

1. Did you have a swim this morning?
2. They don't have their own car!
3. Do you have many public holidays in your country?
4. They have their passports with them.
5. He doesn't have a beard, just a moustache.

23 Frage, Frageanhängsel, Kurzantwort (Question, question tag, short answer)

- Sätze, die ein **primäres** ('be', 'have') **oder modales Hilfsverb** ('can', 'could', 'will', 'would', 'must' etc.) enthalten, bilden **Fragen** durch **Umstellung** (Inversion) von Subjekt und Hilfsverb, z.B.

  Are we staying much longer? *Can you help me?*
  Have they been on holiday? *Must I leave?*

- Sätze, die **kein primäres oder modales Hilfsverb** enthalten, bilden **Fragen** mit **'do'/'does'/'did',** z.B.

  Do you like spinach? *Where did they go?*
  What does he think? *Why didn't he ring her?*

- Auch Sätze mit den **Vollverben 'to do' und 'to have'** (s. unit 14) bilden **Fragen** mit **'do'/'does'/'did',** z.B.

  Do you do your homework at the weekend?
  Does she have lunch in the office?

- In positiven sog. **‚Subjektfragen',** in denen das Fragewort Subjekt des Satzes ist, verwendet man **kein 'do'/'does'/'did',** z.B.

  Who knows the rules? (aber: *Who doesn't know the rules?*)
  Which of you plays tennis? (aber: *Which of you doesn't play tennis?*)

- Es gibt im Englischen keine direkte Entsprechung für das deutsche ‚nicht wahr?', ‚oder?' und ‚nicht?'. Das **Frageanhängsel** im Englischen richtet sich nach dem **Verb des vorausgehenden Satzes.** Wie bei der Bildung von Fragen und Kurzantworten spielen hier die Hilfsverben die entscheidende Rolle. Sowohl die primären als auch die modalen Hilfsverben werden im Frageanhängsel wieder aufgenommen. Auf einen **bejahten Satz** folgt i.d.R. ein **verneintes Frageanhängsel** und umgekehrt.

+ –	– +
We were here tonight, weren't we?	*You don't eat meat, do you?*
You can dance, can't you?	*He hasn't stolen before, has he?*

Besonderheiten:

Let's	*Let's sit down, shall we?*	**shall we?**
Aufforderung	*Help yourself to tea, will you?*	**will you?**
I'm	*I'm very lucky, aren't I?*	**aren't I?**

- Die bloße Antwort 'yes' oder 'no' wirkt im Englischen oft unfreundlich. Man bevorzugt deshalb **Kurzantworten,** die das **Hilfsverb** aus der Frage **wieder aufgreifen,** z. B.

Do you live here? - *Yes, I do. Just around the corner actually.*
Are you German? - *No, I'm not. I'm Austrian.*
Didn't you see me? - *No, I didn't. I'm sorry.*

23 Exercises

I. Turn these statements into questions.

1. We must leave now.
2. She's working in the States.
3. He took a taxi.
4. They can speak English fluently.
5. We've been living here for a long time.
6. Health is more important than wealth.
7. They had to go by car.
8. It looks like it's going to be a nice day.

II. Finish off the short answer. ●●

1. Do you like travelling? Yes, I … .
2. Was she tired? No, she … .
3. Do they have to go? Yes, they … .
4. Will he be joining us later? No, he … .
5. Have they chosen somebody? No, they … .
6. Are you pleased to have finished? Yes, we … .
7. Were they thinking of coming? Yes, they … .
8. Did they call you? No, they … .

III. Add the question tag to complete the question. ●●

1. You're German, …?
2. He's been here before, …?
3. She doesn't work in this company, …?
4. You'd been waiting, …?
5. I don't sound aggressive, …?
6. You were sitting on this seat, …?
7. Come in, …?
8. We're ready to start, …?

24 Verbformen (Verb forms)

- Im Englischen kann man mit der Form des Verbs zweierlei ausdrücken:
  → **wann** eine Handlung geschieht, geschah bzw. geschehen wird und
  → **wie** diese Handlung vom Sprechenden betrachtet wird, wurde bzw. werden wird, z. B. als regelmäßige oder auf kurze Zeit begrenzte Handlung.

- Für diese zwei Komponenten des Verbs hat das Englische, im Gegensatz zum Deutschen, zwei ‚Systeme' vorgesehen: **für das ‚Wann' das Tempus** ('tense') und **für das ‚Wie' den Aspekt** ('aspect' = 'a way of looking at sth').
  Die Wahl der richtigen Verbform ist also deshalb so schwierig, weil sie nicht nur vom Zeitpunkt des Geschehens abhängt, sondern auch von Sichtweise und Einstellung des Sprechenden mitbestimmt wird.

- Im Englischen unterscheidet man außerdem zwischen **'time'** (= reale Zeit) und **'tense'** (= Tempus, *grammatikalische Bezeichnung*).
  Um etwa eine **gegenwärtige Handlung** zu beschreiben, benötigt man nicht unbedingt eine Gegenwartsform des Verbs. Auch eine **Vergangenheitsform** kann diese Funktion übernehmen, z. B.

  If I had the time, I would go on holiday.

- **Verbformen:**

present simple	*I work*
present continuous	*I am working*
past simple	*I worked*
past continuous	*I was working*
present perfect simple	*I have worked*
present perfect continuous	*I have been working*
past perfect simple	*I had worked*
past perfect continuous	*I had been working*
future simple	*I will work*
future continuous	*I will be working*
future perfect simple	*I will have worked*
future perfect continuous	*I will have been working*

(Diese Verbformen werden in den units 25ff. u. 34f. ausführlich behandelt.)

24 Exercises

I. Don't mix up the concepts of 'time' and 'tense'. Time is a real-world concept. Tense is a grammatical concept. Write down what time (present, past, future) is expressed and what verb form is used in the following sentences.

1. I was wondering if you could help me?
2. We've been living here for five years now.
3. If one day I won a lot of money, I'd give some to you.
4. Did you manage to speak to him?
5. Just imagine that we hadn't got married!

Time	Tense

II. Are four, six or eight of the following verbs in the continuous form?

1. I'm trying hard to concentrate.
2. Have you been watching television?
3. Looking at old photographs is great fun.
4. Did you get the message on the answerphone?
5. She's getting married in July.
6. Will you be coming with us tomorrow?
7. He hasn't done much driving recently.
8. I wouldn't wait if I were you.

III. How many of the following sentences contain verbs which are perfect forms?

1. I've told you so many times before not to do that!
2. Have you seen this film?
3. I'll have reached her by tomorrow evening.
4. He'd left the party before we arrived.
5. She hasn't been feeling well today.
6. They'd known about it before we did.
7. It's been raining all afternoon.
8. I'll have read the paper in ten minutes.

25 Die einfache Form der Gegenwart (The present simple)

Die einfache Form der Gegenwart bezeichnet eine **allgemein gültige Tatsache oder Gewohnheit.**

I	***live***
you	***live***
he, she, it	**lives**
we	***live***
you	***live***
they	***live***

In der **dritten Person Einzahl** erhält das Verb die **Endung -s oder -es,** z.B.

He watches and she speaks.

- **Fragen, Verneinungen** und **Kurzantworten** werden mit dem Hilfsverb **'do'/'does'** gebildet, z.B.

  Do you work here?
  They don't smoke.
  Does he drive? - Yes, he does.

- **Häufigkeitsadverbien** ('frequency adverbs'), wie **'always', 'often', 'sometimes', 'rarely'** und **'never',** sind **Signalwörter** für die einfache Form der Gegenwart, weil sie gewohnheitsmäßige Handlungen beschreiben.
  Bei ihrer Verwendung muss man die Wortstellung beachten: Die Adverbien stehen **vor dem Vollverb** (= 'pre-verb adverbs'), z.B.

  He sometimes visits his parents on Sunday.
  She doesn't usually work at the weekend.

- **Ausnahme 'be':**
  Hier werden **Fragen** durch **Umstellen** von Subjekt und Verb gebildet; zur **Verneinung** verwendet man **'not',** z.B.

  Are you from England?
  We are not happy with the service.

  Häufigkeitsadverbien stehen, wie im Deutschen, **nach 'be',** z.B.

  They are rarely late.

25 Exercises

I. Complete these sentences using the present simple form of the words in brackets. ●●

1. He (know) what she (like).
2. She (say) that her brothers (be) older than she (be).
3. I (like) cooking but I (not, like) washing-up afterwards.
4. He still (go) to school although he (be) nineteen now.
5. We (not, have got) a car because we (not, can) drive.
6. Although they (work) hard, they (not, earn) very much.
7. She (not, drink) coffee. She (prefer) tea.
8. He (not, be) a specialist really. I (think) he (be) more of an all-rounder.

II. What questions must you ask to get the information which is missing?

1. The word ‚Bauchredner' in German means .?. in English.
2. He gets home at .?. every evening – except Friday.
3. She doesn't live in Camden Town anymore. She lives in .?. .
4. He hasn't got a car and there is no bus service so he gets to school by .?. .
5. He speaks so loudly all the time because .?. .
6. This pen isn't mine. It's .?. . She had it with her this morning.
7. They see .?. every weekend throughout the whole year.
8. Don't be silly! Her eyes are not blue. They're .?. !

III. Put the adverbs of frequency into the right position. ●●

1. We are in England.	(often)
2. We fly there.	(usually)
3. We go to London.	(sometimes)
4. We stay there for a week.	(normally)
5. We would stay in big hotels.	(never)
6. They are far too expensive.	(usually)

*IV. A pronunciation problem. Which verb is the odd one out (*nicht zugehörig*)? Why?* ●●

1. go	→	goes
2. eat	→	eats
3. say	→	says
4. work	→	works
5. fly	→	flys

26 Die Verlaufsform der Gegenwart (The present continuous)

I	**am**	
you	***are***	
he, she, it	**is**	***learning***
we	***are***	
you	***are***	
they	***are***	

Die Verlaufsform der Gegenwart wird gebildet aus einer Form von **'to be' + -ing-Form** des Verbs.

- Die **Frageform** wird durch **Umstellen** von Subjekt und jeweiliger Form von 'to be' gebildet; zur **Verneinung** verwendet man **'not',** z. B.

  Are you having breakfast?
  They're not talking to each other.

- Im gesprochenen Englisch werden i.d.R. Personalpronomen und jeweilige Form von 'to be' **zusammengezogen,** z. B.

  I'm listening. (statt: *I am listening.*)
  They're coming. (statt: *They are coming.*)

Im Allgemeinen kommen Verlaufsformen viel weniger vor als einfache Formen. Dennoch ist ihr richtiger **Gebrauch** für Lernende schwieriger (s. unit 33):

- Die Verlaufsform der Gegenwart beschreibt eine **zum Zeitpunkt des Sprechens ablaufende Handlung,** z. B.

  Don't disturb me, please. I'm working.

- Auch für Ereignisse und Handlungen, die während einer **begrenzten Zeitspanne** stattfinden, wird die Verlaufsform verwendet, z. B.

  I'm staying with my parents until I can find a new flat.

- Sie kann sich als Gegenwartsform auf eine **zukünftige Situation** beziehen (s. unit 37), z. B.

  We're having a holiday in the USA next summer.

26 Exercises

I. Use the correct form of the words in brackets to complete these mini-dialogues. ●●

1. Are you OK?
   Yes. I … (try) to think.
2. Who … (make) all that noise?
   It's only our neighbours.
3. Excuse me. We … (look) for a post office.
   Yes. There's one just around the corner.
4. Where's Mike?
   He … (not, work) in the garden so he must be indoors somewhere.
5. What's the matter?
   It … (snow)! In the middle of May!

II. In which of the following sentences does the continuous form describe an action at the moment of speaking?

1. Prices are rising.
2. Is the world's population increasing?
3. Your English is getting much better.
4. What are you doing here at this time of day?
5. I'm reading a fascinating book at the moment.

III. Complete this dialogue using the correct form of the words in brackets. ●●

Clare: Hi, Rick. What … (you, do) these days?
Rick: I … (study).
Clare: And what … (you, study)?
Rick: Maths.
Clare: Maths! … (you, enjoy) the course?
Rick: It's not too bad. I … (learn) a lot. Yourself?
Clare: I … (apply) for jobs at the moment.
Rick: And? What are the chances?
Clare: I … (not, think) they're very good.
Rick: Why's that?
Clare: The companies … (not, want) people like me. I'm overqualified!

27 Die einfache Form der Vergangenheit (The past simple)

Die einfache Form der Vergangenheit bezeichnet einen **in der Vergangenheit abgeschlossenen Vorgang.** Sie wird v.a. in Erzählungen, Berichten und rasch aufeinander folgenden sog. ‚Kettenhandlungen' verwendet.

I	
you	
he, she, it	***asked***
we	
you	
they	

- Die einfache Form der Vergangenheit der **regelmäßigen Verben** bildet man durch **Anhängen von -ed** an die Grundform des Verbs.

  Regeln zur Schreibung:

stop	→	*stopped*	(Endkonsonant nach kurzem, betonten Vokal verdoppelt)
cry	→	*cried*	(-y nach Konsonant zu -ied)
hate	→	*hated*	(stummes -e am Ende entfällt)

- Die **unregelmäßigen Verben** bilden eine **eigene Form.** Die wenigsten, aber gebräuchlichsten Verben im Englischen sind unregelmäßig (s. S. 133ff.), z.B.

be	***was, were***	*make*	***made***
begin	***began***	*put*	***put***
do	***did***	*see*	***saw***
go	***went***	*take*	***took***
have	***had***	*tell*	***told***
keep	***kept***	*think*	***thought***

- **Fragen** werden mit **'did'** und der Grundform des Verbs gebildet; bei **Verneinungen** kommt **'not'** hinzu, z.B.

  Did you phone him? *We didn't see them.*

- **Ausnahme 'be':**
  Fragen werden durch **Umstellen** von Subjekt und 'was'/'were' gebildet, z.B.

  Were you on holiday in August? – Yes, we were.

27 Exercises

I. Complete the mini-dialogues using the correct form of the verb in brackets. (They are all irregular verbs!) ●●

1. Why was your arm so red this morning?
   Something … (bite) me in the night.
2. Are you hungry?
   No, thanks. I … (have) a very big lunch earlier.
3. Where's Amelia?
   I don't know. I … (see) her a second ago.
4. There's no more milk.
   I'm sorry. I … (drink) it all last night.
5. You're not tired, are you?
   No, I … (sleep) very well yesterday.

II. Make questions in the past simple to match the answers. (Some of the words have been given.) ●●

1. Where … last night?	To the cinema.
2. How … there?	By bus.
3. What …?	The new James Bond film.
4. Did …?	Yes, we did. It was good fun and quite funny in parts.
5. Why … late?	Because we went to have something to eat afterwards.

III. Complete the fable using the past tense of the verbs in brackets. ●●

A fox … (see) a crow in a tree. The crow … (have) a piece of cheese in her mouth. The fox … (be) hungry so he … (think) for a minute and then … (speak): 'Hello, my dear crow. You are pretty! What beautiful feathers! You must have a lovely voice. Please sing.'

The stupid crow … (like) what she … (hear) and she … (begin) to sing. At that moment the cheese (fall) … out of her mouth. The fox … (catch) it and … (eat) it immediately. Then he … (laugh) and … (run) away.

The moral of the story: Don't be fooled by flattery (*Schmeicheleien*).

28 Die Verlaufsform der Vergangenheit (The past continuous)

I	***was***	
you	***were***	
he, she, it	***was***	***playing***
we	***were***	
you	***were***	
they	***were***	

Die Verlaufsform der Vergangenheit wird gebildet aus **'was'/'were' + -ing-Form** des Verbs.

- Die **Frageform** wird durch **Umstellen** von 'was'/'were' gebildet; zur Bildung der **Verneinung** verwendet man **'not',** z.B.

  Were you speaking to somebody?
  I wasn't listening.

- Die Verlaufsform der Vergangenheit betont, im Unterschied zur einfachen Form, dass ein **Vorgang in der Vergangenheit längere Zeit angedauert** hat, z.B.

  We were cycling through the village.

- Sie beschreibt, dass **zu einem bestimmten Zeitpunkt in der Vergangenheit etwas im Gange** war. Im Deutschen kann man in solchen Sätzen oft **‚gerade'** hinzufügen, z.B.

  What were you doing at three o'clock? – We were swimming.
  (Wir waren gerade Schwimmen.)

- Die Verlaufsform der Vergangenheit wird häufig **zusammen mit der einfachen Form** gebraucht. Die Verlaufsform drückt dabei aus, dass eine Handlung (die sog. **‚Hintergrundhandlung'**) bereits ablief, während eine neue und wichtigere (in der einfachen Form) eingetreten ist, z.B.

  We were cycling through the village when we saw a terrible accident.

- Wie bei allen Verlaufsformen ist die Bildung der Verlaufsform der Vergangenheit **mit sog. ‚Zustandsverben'** (s. unit 33) **selten.**

28 Exercises

*I. There was a small earthquake (*Erdbeben*) in Aberdeen last year. What were the following people doing when they felt it? Complete the sentences using the verbs in brackets in the past continuous.*

1. Alex … (have) a drink in the pub.
2. Robert and Stephen … (play) football.
3. Catherine … (drive) home from the office.
4. Malcolm … (lie) in bed with a bad headache.
5. Anna and Carol … (argue) about money.
6. Jane … (sit) at her PC and … (write) a letter to her bank manager.
7. Jill and Tom … (watch) a thriller on TV.
8. Paul … (mow, *mähen*) the lawn (*Rasen*).

II. Use these prompts (‚Helfer‘*) to formulate questions in the past continuous.* ●●

1. where/you/live/five years ago?
2. you/live/alone?
3. you/work/at that time?
4. you/do/the job/you wanted?
5. you/earn/enough money?
6. you/enjoy/life/as much as now?

III. In each sentence two verbs are missing: one in the past simple and one in the past continuous. Add them. ●●

1. I … (travel) home yesterday when I … (meet) Simon at the station.
2. … (you, sit) in the garden when we … (phone)?
3. What … (you, laugh) about when I … (come) in?
4. While we … (wait) for the bus it … (begin) to rain.
5. They … (get) married while they … (live) in Seattle.
6. Somebody … (steal) all my money while I … (shop) in London.
7. She … (leave) the house when the phone … (ring).
8. I … (fall) asleep when my children … (come) in and … (wake) me up.

IV. Complete this passage from a novel by using past tense forms of the verbs in brackets. (Only one of the verbs is in the past continuous form.) ●●

'I … (go) to the bar and … (get) the beer and … (carry) it outside and … (wander) down the garden towards the pool. It … (be) a fine garden with lawns and beds of azaleas and tall coconut palm trees and the wind … (blow) strongly through the tops of the palm trees.'

(From *Man from the South* by Roald Dahl)

29 Die einfache Form des Perfekts (The present perfect simple)

I	***have***	***seen***
you	***have***	
he, she, it	**has**	
we	***have***	
you	***have***	
they	***have***	

Die einfache Form des Perfekts bildet man mit dem Hilfsverb **'have'/'has' + Partizip Perfekt** (dritte Form des Verbs, 'past participle').

- **Fragen** werden durch **Umstellen** gebildet; zur **Verneinung** verwendet man **'not',** z.B.

  Have you seen her today? *She has not found it.*

- 'have + not' bzw. 'has + not' wird in der gesprochenen Sprache üblicherweise **zusammengezogen,** z.B.

  We haven't met before.

- Das Present Perfect ist keine reine Vergangenheitsform, sondern eine ‚Brücke' zwischen Vergangenheit und Gegenwart. Es interessiert weniger der Zeitpunkt des Geschehens, als vielmehr seine **Auswirkungen auf die Gegenwart.**

- **Signalwörter** für Present Perfect, z.B. JENNY …

just	*We've just called you.*	(gerade)
ever	*Have you ever been to Canada?*	(jemals)
never	*I've never had my name in the paper.*	(nie)
not … yet	*She hasn't told him yet.*	(noch nicht)
yet	*Have you heard from her yet?*	(schon)

- Für Vorgänge, die **in der Vergangenheit begonnen** haben und **bis in die Gegenwart andauern,** wird gleichfalls Present Perfect verwendet. Häufig steht in solchen Fällen **'for'** bzw. **'since',** z.B.

We've been here for three hours.	***for***	**Zeitraum**
We've been here since lunchtime.	***since***	**Zeitpunkt**

29 Exercises

I. Answer the following questions using the present perfect simple of the verb in brackets. Add any other words not provided.

1. Would you like a cup of tea? (just, have, one)
2. Do you know Peter at all? (know, him, for years)
3. Is your leg OK? (pull, a muscle)
4. Are you new here? (be, here, for six months)
5. Why are you smiling? (just, pass, my exams)
6. Where's your car? (sell, to a friend)
7. Why are you going to London? (never, be, there, before)
8. What do you think of Graham Swift's new book? (not, read, it, yet)

II. Add 'for' or 'since' to complete these sentences.

1. We've been married … 1989.
2. Have you lived here … long?
3. She's gone away … a week.
4. Have they been here … the beginning of the year?
5. We've known each other … we were children.
6. He's had a cold … weeks now.
7. She hasn't contacted us … Christmas.
8. Have they said anything … they arrived?

III. Translate the following sentences into good English.

1. Wir sind gerade angekommen.
2. Ich habe den Film noch nicht gesehen.
3. Waren Sie schon einmal in Cornwall?
4. Den Witz habe ich schon einmal gehört!
5. Wir sind noch nie durch den Kanaltunnel gefahren.

IV. What's the difference in meaning?

1. How long are you here for?
2. How long have you been here for?

30 Die Verlaufsform des Perfekts (The present perfect continuous)

I	***have***	
you	***have***	
he, she, it	**has**	***been waiting***
we	***have***	
you	***have***	
they	***have***	

Die Verlaufsform des Perfekts wird aus **'have'/'has' + 'been' + -ing-Form** des Verbs gebildet.

- **Fragen** werden durch **Umstellen** gebildet; zur **Verneinung** verwendet man **'not',** z. B.

  Have you been standing here long?
  I have not been lying here long.

- Die Verlaufsform des Perfekts drückt aus, dass eine **Handlung noch nicht beendet** ist oder **eben erst beendet** wurde, z. B.

  Who's been drinking my tea?

- Betont wird das **Andauern** einer Handlung (mit **'for'** bzw. **'since'**), nicht ihr Ergebnis, z. B.

  We've been living here for over twenty years now.

- Die Verlaufsform des Perfekts drückt oft eine **emotional gefärbte Aussage** aus, z. B.

  I've been sitting here for an hour and nobody's even said 'hello'!

30 Exercises

I. When the three bears come back home from their walk in the wood they discover that Goldilocks has been in their house. What questions do they ask? Use the prompts to complete them! ●●

1. Who/eat/my porridge?
2. Who/sit/my chair?
3. Who/sleep/my bed?

II. Baby Bear's porridge, chair and bed are very popular with Goldilocks. What does Baby Bear say? Use the prompts to complete the sentences. (You need one continuous form and two simple forms of the present perfect!) ●●

1. Somebody/eat/all my porridge!
2. Somebody/break/my chair!
3. Somebody/sleep/my bed/and/she/be/still/there!

III. Match the sentences with the correct 'meaning'.

1. Have you seen Sophie? 2. Have you been seeing Sophie?	a. this morning b. over the last few weeks
3. She's learnt French. 4. She's been learning French.	a. she has not finished yet b. she's learning Spanish now
5. He's had problems with his back. 6. He's been having problems with his back.	a. his back is still a problem b. his back is better now
7. I haven't bought a paper. 8. I haven't been buying a paper.	a. I had no time this morning b. I don't want a paper anymore
9. They haven't spoken to me. 10. They haven't been speaking to me.	a. some time ago but not recently b. never

31 Die einfache Form der Vorvergangenheit (The past perfect simple)

I	
you	
he, she, it	***had driven***
we	
you	
they	

Die einfache Form der Vorvergangenheit bildet man mit dem Hilfsverb **'had' + Partizip Perfekt.**

- Wie beim Perfekt werden **Fragen** durch **Umstellen** gebildet; zur **Verneinung** verwendet man **'not',** z. B.

  Had he left before you arrived? *We had not gone far.*

- Im gesprochenen Englisch werden Personalpronomen und Hilfsverb 'had' üblicherweise **zusammengezogen,** z. B.

  Nobody realized what he'd said.

- Die einfache Form der Vorvergangenheit beschreibt Handlungen oder Vorgänge, die, wie der Name sagt, **vor der Vergangenheit** stattfanden, z. B.

  When we got to the station the train had already left.

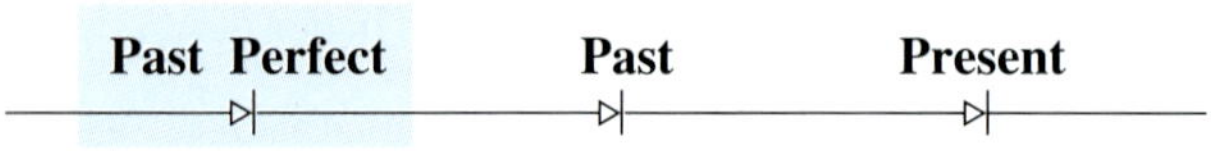

- Die einfache Form der Vorvergangenheit wird oft **zusammen mit der einfachen Form der Vergangenheit** verwendet, um auszudrücken, dass eine erste Handlung vor einer zweiten, jeweils in der Vergangenheit, stattfand.
  Den Zeitunterschied zwischen beiden Handlungen signalisieren oft Wörter wie **'after', 'already', 'because', 'before', 'so'** oder **'when',** z. B.

  I didn't go to the cinema because I'd seen the film before.

- Die Formen der Vorvergangenheit finden häufig Anwendung bei der **indirekten Rede** (s. unit 44f.), z. B.

  They said that they had met us before.

31 Exercises

I. Join the half-sentences 1–5 to half-sentences a–e. Complete them by using the past perfect simple form. ●●

1. The restaurant was no longer open		a. I … (never, met) her before.
2. It was difficult to talk to her		b. it … (close) at midnight.
3. We weren't able to talk to them	because	c. the bus … (be) late.
4. We missed the first act of the play		d. I … (never, fly) before.
5. I felt a bit nervous		e. they (already, go) home.

II. Which words from the box below link the half-sentences best?

after • as • because • before • when

1. We took a picture of the sea just … the sun had come up.
2. She had already left the office … her husband rang.
3. He could speak perfect English … he had lived in England for five years.
4. They had learnt about the dangers of bungee jumping … they were allowed to jump themselves.
5. The training course was not … hard as the participants had expected.

III. To complete this passage from a novel you need five past simple forms, one past continuous form and two past perfect simple forms of the verbs in brackets. ●●

'This … (be) an important journey for Mrs Foster. She … (go) all alone to Paris to visit her daughter, her only child, who … (be married) to a Frenchman. Mrs Foster … (not, care) for the Frenchman much, but she … (be) fond of her daughter, and, more than that, she … (develop) a great yearning (*Sehnsucht*) to set eyes on her three grandchildren. She … (know) them only from the many photographs she … (receive).'

(From *The Way up to Heaven* by Roald Dahl)

32 Die Verlaufsform der Vorvergangenheit (The past perfect continuous)

Die Verlaufsform der Vorvergangenheit betont den **Verlauf** einer Handlung, die **vor der Vergangenheit** stattfand.

I *you* *he, she, it* *we* *you* *they*	***had been running***

Die Verlaufsform der Vorvergangenheit wird mit **'had' + 'been' + -ing-Form** des Verbs gebildet.

- **Fragen** erhält man durch **Umstellen,** z. B.

  How long had you been studying before you had a child?

- Zur Bildung der **Verneinung** verwendet man **'not',** z. B.

  She had not been working for very long when the computer crashed.

32 Exercises

I. Explain the situations by forming sentences in the past perfect continuous. ●●

1. Why was there such a terrible smell when we walked into the room?
   A lot of people/smoke.
2. Why didn't Kathy know where she was when she woke up?
   She/dream.
3. Why did Rick have wet feet when he came home?
   He/cycle/in the rain.
4. Why were Tony and Pete so red in the face?
   They/run.
5. Why did Tracy know so much about French impressionists?
   She/read/a book about them.

II. Match the sentences with their 'meanings' (a–b).

1. When I left the plane it was snowing.	a. snow was falling
2. When I left the plane it had been snowing.	b. snow was on the ground
3. When they saw him he was drinking.	a. he had a full glass in his hand
4. When they saw him he had been drinking.	b. there was an empty glass
5. When we arrived they were arguing.	a. they were not talking to each other
6. When we arrived they had been arguing.	b. they were shouting at each other
7. When she came in he was smoking.	a. there was smoke in the room
8. When she came in he had been smoking.	b. he had a cigarette in his mouth

III. Read the situation and then write a sentence using the past perfect continuous form. (Start your sentences with 'After …'.) ●●

1. The plane was flying to Orlando, Florida. After an hour there was an engine failure.
2. He was driving to England. After eight hours he fell asleep at the steering wheel and crashed.
3. She was cycling to work. After forty minutes she got cramp in her leg and had to stop.
4. They were trying to hitchhike to Wales. After two minutes somebody picked them up.
5. We were playing loud music in the garden. After two hours the neighbour complained about the noise.
6. The children were reading together. After ten minutes an argument broke out.

33 Zustandsverben (Stative verbs)

- Im Englischen gibt es sowohl einfache Formen als auch Verlaufsformen des Verbs (s. units 24ff. u. 34f.). Die **Verlaufsform** ist eine Besonderheit der englischen Grammatik, die oft Schwierigkeiten bereitet. Durch ihren Gebrauch bringt der Sprechende zum Ausdruck, dass er eine **Handlung als zeitlich begrenzt oder als nicht abgeschlossen** betrachtet.

- Die sog. **‚Zustandsverben'** findet man **selten** in der **Verlaufsform,** weil sie **permanente Zustände,** und **keine echten Handlungen,** beschreiben.
  Zu den wichtigsten Zustandsverben gehören die **Verben** des **Glaubens** (**1**), der **Empfindung** (**2**), der **Sinneswahrnehmung** (**3**) und des **Besitzens** (**4**):

1. Glauben		**2. Empfindung**	
to believe	(glauben)	***to hate***	(hassen)
to know	(wissen)	***to like***	(mögen)
to mean	(bedeuten)	***to love***	(lieben)
to think	(denken, glauben)	***to need***	(brauchen)
to understand	(verstehen)	***to want***	(wollen)
3. Sinne		**4. Besitz**	
to feel	(spüren)	***to belong to***	(gehören)
to hear	(hören)	***to consist of***	(bestehen aus)
to look	(aussehen)	***to contain***	(beinhalten)
to see	(sehen, wahrnehmen)	***to depend on***	(abhängen von)
to smell	(riechen)	***to have***	(haben, besitzen)
to sound	(klingen)	***to own***	(besitzen)
to taste	(schmecken)	***to possess***	(besitzen)

- Die meisten der o.g. Verben haben **weitere Bedeutungen** und können als sog. **‚dynamische Verben'** auch in der **Verlaufsform** verwendet werden, z.B.

I think Indian food is lovely.	(denken, finden)
I'm thinking about emigrating.	(s. überlegen zu, nachdenken über)

33 Exercises

I. In the following pairs of sentences only one sentence is possible. Which one is it?

1. a. She comes from Manchester and she still lives there.
   b. She is coming from Manchester and she still lives there.

2. a. What is this expression meaning?
   b. What does this expression mean?

3. a. We like coffee.
   b. We are liking coffee.

4. a. I believe everything you said.
   b. I am believing everything you said.

II. Complete these sentences using the correct form of the words in brackets. ●●

1. Watch out! This jar … (contain) petrol.
2. Those glasses … (look) very old. Are they old?
3. She … (hate) bitter but she … (not, mind) lager.
4. … (anyone, want) more potatoes?
5. Which part of the States … (she, come) from exactly? East coast?
6. … (you, really, love) me?
7. I … (not, understand) what you … (mean). Can you repeat what you said?
8. We … (want) a holiday but we … (not, want) an expensive one.

III. Complete these pairs of sentences by using the correct form of the words in brackets. (One verb form is present simple and the other is present continuous.) ●●

1. You look worried. What … (you, think) about?
2. What … (you, think) of classical music?

3. … (your brother, have) black hair?
4. … (your brother, have) a party next week?

5. We … (look) tired because we had a late night last night.
6. We … (look) for a new flat. Any tips?

7. … (he, see) his parents very often these days?
8. … (he, see) the difference between them?

34 Zukunftsformen I (Future forms I)

1. **'will'** (***modales Hilfsverb***) **+ Infinitiv,** z.B.
   I'll see you later.
2. **'to be going to' + Infinitiv,** z.B.
   She's going to have a baby in April.
3. **Present Simple,** z.B.
   The plane leaves at 9.45 this morning.
4. **Present Continuous,** z.B.
   I am starting a new job next week.

Zu den **gebräuchlichsten Zukunftsformen** gehören die Formen 'will' + Infinitiv (**1**), 'to be going to' + Infinitiv (**2**) sowie die beiden Gegenwartsformen (**3/4**).

- Als **Hilfsverb** wird **'will'** (**1**) verwendet, um die **Meinung und Einstellung** des Sprechenden **zum Zeitpunkt des Sprechens** auszudrücken (s. units 17 u. 36), z.B.

  I'll have a cup of tea. (Ich nehme eine Tasse Tee.)

- **'to be going to'** (**2**) wird verwendet, um bereits gefasste **Absichten oder in Gang gesetzte Ereignisse** zum Ausdruck zu bringen, z.B.

  It's going to rain. (… denn der Himmel ist stark bewölkt.)

- **Present Simple** (**3**) drückt aus, dass ein zukünftiges Geschehen **von außen,** durch **Fahrpläne, Programme** oder **Öffnungszeiten,** festgelegt wurde, z.B.

  The bank closes at 3.30 this afternoon, doesn't it?

- **Present Continuous** (**4**) steht bei festen **eigenen Plänen, Vereinbarungen** oder **Terminen,** z.B.

  We're having our summer holiday in Greece.

34 Exercises

I. Which sentence below would be the appropriate reply to the following statement? ●●

'Wow! Sally's put on a lot of weight!'

1. No, she'll have a baby!
2. No, she will be having a baby!
3. No, she's going to have a baby!
4. No, she has a baby!

II. Which sentence would be the most suitable reply to the following question?

'Are you busy on Friday night?'

1. Yes, we will be dancing.
2. Yes, we will dance.
3. Yes, we will have danced.
4. Yes, we're dancing.

III. Which sentence below would be a polite way of replying to the waiter's question? ●●

'Can I get you anything to drink?'

1. A gin and tonic. OK?
2. I'll have a gin and tonic, please.
3. I have a gin and tonic, please.
4. I'll be having a gin and tonic, please.

*IV. At the beginning of the year people often make a New Year's resolution (*Vorsatz*). Which of the following sentences sounds like a New Year's resolution?*

1. I will get fit.
2. I'm going to get fit.
3. I get fit.
4. I will have got fit.

35 Zukunftsformen II (Future forms II)

Es gibt eine Reihe anderer Verbformen, die zukünftige Ereignisse ausdrücken, z. B.

1. **'will' (*nicht modales Hilfsverb*) + Infinitiv,** z. B.

   The minister will visit Spain next week.

2. **'will' + 'be' + -ing-Form** des Verbs, z. B.

   We will be arriving at ten o'clock.

3. **'will' + 'have' + Partizip Perfekt,** z.B.

   Soon they will have built a motorway here.

4. **'will' + 'have been' + -ing-Form** des Verbs, z.B.

   By May she will have been working here for one year.

- **Future Simple (nicht modales 'will' + Infinitiv (1))** wird verwendet, um **sachlich** und **objektiv** von zukünftigen Ereignissen zu sprechen, z. B.

  The Euro will become Europe's currency.

- **Future Continuous (2)** beschreibt eine Handlung, die zu einem **bestimmten Zeitpunkt ablaufen** wird, z. B.

  They will be staying with us for a week.

- **Future Perfect Simple (3)** bezieht sich auf eine zu einem **bestimmten Zeitpunkt in der Zukunft abgeschlossene Handlung,** z. B.

  If we don't hurry up, the show will have started.

- **Future Perfect Continuous (4)** verdeutlicht, dass eine Handlung zu einem **bestimmten Zeitpunkt in der Zukunft noch andauern** wird. Man verwendet dazu **Zeitpartikel** für Zeitraum bzw. Zeitpunkt, z. B.

  In two years' time we will have been living here for over 25 years.

35 Exercises

I. Three of these sentences contain a non-modal 'will'. One doesn't. Which is it?

1. There will be rain in England and most parts of Wales.
2. We'll call you from the airport.
3. Mr Palmer will be sixty-five next year.
4. The Euro will become Europe's currency.

Non-modal 'will'	Modal 'will'

II. Make these sentences sound more polite by using the future continuous form of the verb.

1. I'll ring them at six.
2. Will she wait for you?
3. We'll arrive just after ten.
4. Will you spend the night in a hotel?

III. Use the future perfect simple form of the verb in brackets to complete the sentences. ●●

1. If we don't get to the shops soon they … (close). Come on! Hurry up!
2. I … (spend) all the extra money I earned by the middle of the month.
3. She … (finish) her course by next summer, won't she?
4. When you come back home from a year abroad you … (learn) a lot.

IV. Use the future perfect continuous form of the verb in brackets to complete these sentences. ●●

1. In four months from now I … (do) this course for five years.
2. By this time tomorrow you … (drive) for more than twenty-four hours!
3. In two months' time they … (live) in their flat for thirty years.
4. By the end of the week he … (work) on his book for a whole year.

V. Read this text with a dictionary. ●●

Cowards die many times before their deaths;
The valiant never taste of death but once.
Of all the wonders that I yet have heard
It seems to me most strange that men should fear;
Seeing that death, a necessary end,
Will come when it will come.

(From *Julius Caesar* by William Shakespeare)

36 'going to' & 'will' + Infinitiv (infinitive)

I	**am**		*I*	
you	***are***		*you*	
he, she, it	**is**	***going to see***	*he, she, it*	***will see***
we	***are***		*we*	
you	***are***		*you*	
they	***are***		*they*	

Das sog. **'going to-future'** wird mit einer Form von **'to be' + 'going to' + Infinitiv** gebildet.

- Die **Frageform** erhält man durch **Umstellen** von 'to be' und Subjekt; zur **Verneinung** verwendet man **'not',** z. B.

  Are you going to come or not?
  We're not going to have a pay rise this year.

- Das **'going to-future'** wird verwendet, um bereits **gefasste Absichten oder in Gang gesetzte Ereignisse** auszudrücken. Für den Sprechenden ist das **Zukünftige** bereits in der Gegenwart **erkennbar.** Deshalb wird diese Form auch als **'present-future'** bezeichnet.

Es gibt **zwei Arten von 'will'**: ein modales und ein nicht modales (s. unit 34f.):

- Das modale 'will' drückt die **Meinung und Einstellung** des Sprechenden **zum Zeitpunkt des Sprechens** aus (s. units 17 u. 34). Dieses 'will' nennt man **'spontaneous will'.** Im Deutschen stehen die meist schnellen und unüberlegten Reaktionen in der Gegenwartsform, z. B.

  I'll call you back. (Ich rufe dich zurück.)

- Weniger gebräuchlich als das modale 'will' ist das nicht modale **'neutral will'** (s. unit 35). Auch als **'neutral future'** bezeichnet, benötigt man diese Zukunftsform, um **sachlich und emotionslos über zukünftige Ereignisse** zu sprechen, z. B.

  The unions' talks with the government will begin next Monday.

Das modale 'will' wird von Lernenden zu selten eingesetzt; das nicht modale 'will' wird häufig überbeansprucht.

36 Exercises

I. In which sentences do you need 'to be going to' and in which do you need 'will'? Add them in the appropriate places in these mini-dialogues. ●●

1. Do you know how this fax machine works?
   Yeah. It's really easy. I … show you.
2. Are you here tomorrow?
   Yes, in the afternoon. I … see you at about two.
3. Are you tired?
   Yes, very. I … go to bed.
4. Did you remember to get some bread?
   Oh no! I forgot! I … get some now.
5. The front door bell just rang.
   Did it? OK. I … get it.
6. We want to change our car.
   Oh yes? What sort … (you/get) next?

II. Which type of 'will' is it? Spontaneous or neutral?

1. I'll take you to the airport if you want.
2. We'll give you a ring next week.
3. The meeting will start at two.
4. Leave it. It won't work.
5. Will you come by train or by coach?
6. I'll get angry if you say that again!

Spon.	Neutral

III. Which sentence in each pair sounds appropriate? Mark it with a cross.

1a. I'll go to the post office for you if you want.
1b. I'm going to go to the post office if you want.

2a. Was that the phone? I'm going to get it.
2b. Was that the phone? I'll get it.

3a. I've got so much work at the moment. I'll work in the office on Sunday.
3b. I've got so much work at the moment. I'm going to work in the office on Sunday.

4a. It's the second time the TV has suddenly broken down. I'll tell them.
4b. It's the second time the TV has suddenly broken down. I'm going to tell them.

5a. She looks very ill so I'll call the doctor.
5b. She looks very ill so I'm going to call the doctor.

37 Gegenwartsformen für Zukunftsereignisse (Present tense forms for future events)

- Die **Verlaufsform der Gegenwart** wird oft verwendet, um bereits **festgelegte Termine, Pläne** oder **Vereinbarungen** auszudrücken (s. unit 34). Meist erscheint dabei eine genaue **Zeitangabe** (z.B. 'next Monday') oder ein **Fragewort der Zeit** ('When?' oder 'What time?').

  Diese Form der Zukunft wird als **'diary future'** ('diary' = Terminkalender) bezeichnet, z.B.

  What are you doing at the weekend?
  They're driving to England on April 25.

- Auch die **einfache Form der Gegenwart** wird verwendet, um über zukünftige Ereignisse zu sprechen. Sie drückt aus, dass ein **zukünftiges Geschehen unbeeinflussbar durch Fahrpläne, Kalender** oder ein **Programm festgelegt** worden ist (s. unit 34).

  Man spricht deshalb von **'timetable future'** ('timetable' = Fahrplan), z.B.

  When does our plane leave exactly?
  The exhibition opens on December 9.

37 Exercises

I. Is it present time or future time? Put a cross in the appropriate column.

	present time	future time
1. Are you feeling OK?		
2. We're leaving in five minutes.		
3. I'm expecting a call from my boss.		
4. They're arriving here on Saturday.		
5. I'm working late every evening this week.		
6. He's getting the 7.05 train.		
7. Are we going out tonight?		
8. Ssh! She's sleeping.		

II. Which questions must you ask to get the information which is missing? (Remember that prepositions can come at the end of questions.) ●●

1. My birthday is on a .?. this year.
2. Many supermarkets in Britain close at .?. in the evening.
3. He's staying at the .?. Hotel. Have you heard of it?
4. There are flights to Philadelphia every .?. in summer.
5. Our train leaves at .?., I think.
6. We're having a holiday with .?. and .?. . Do you know them?
7. .?. is organizing a party at Christmas. Are you going?
8. She's going back to live with her parents because .?. .

III. Complete the text using the correct form of the words in brackets. (Use the present continuous in one paragraph and the present simple in the other.) ●●

'Hello. My name is William and I … (look after) you until Wednesday. I'd like to give you the plan for today. The bus … (pick) us up outside the hotel after breakfast and we … (drive) through London, past Windsor and along the M40 to Oxford. We … (stop) for lunch in Warwick and after a 1-hour break – you may want to look around the castle – we … (carry on) to Stratford-upon-Avon.

Our tour of the Swan Theatre … (begin) at 3 o'clock and … (last) forty-five minutes. Alternatively you can go to the Shakespeare Centre in the middle of town. Afterwards you … (be) free to check into the hotel and do what you wish. The performance tonight … (start) at 7.30. Any questions? Yes? Oh, yes. Tonight it's *All's Well That Ends Well.*'

38 Das Passiv (The passive)

	present	past	present perfect	past perfect	
I	**am**	**was**	***have been***		
you	***are***	***were***	***have been***		
he, she, it	**is**	**was**	**has** ***been***	***had been***	***asked***
we	***are***	***were***	***have been***		
you	***are***	***were***	***have been***		
they	***are***	***were***	***have been***		

Gebildet wird das Passiv mit einer Form von **'to be' + Partizip Perfekt.**

- Das Passiv (Leideform) ermöglicht es, eine Handlung zu beschreiben, **ohne die agierende Person zu nennen:**

	Subjekt	Verb	Objekt	
aktiv	*A man*	*stole*	*£5m*	*from a bank.*
passiv	*£5m*	*were stolen*	*(by a man)*	*from a bank.*

- Sind die handelnden Personen für das Verständnis eines Sachverhalts wichtig, werden sie **mit der Präposition 'by' ergänzt,** z.B.

  He was stopped by the police.

- Bei einigen Verben, wie **'ask', 'give', 'offer', 'send', 'show', 'teach'** oder **'tell',** ist das sog. **‚persönliche Passiv'** sehr gebräuchlich. Hier übernimmt das indirekte Objekt eines Aktivsatzes (*my daughter*) in einem Passivsatz die Funktion des Subjekts, z.B.

  Someone gave my daughter some flowers. (aktiv)
  My daughter was given some flowers. (passiv)

- Viele **‚man'-Sätze** stehen im Englischen im Passiv, z.B.

  I was given the smallest office. (Man hat mir … gegeben.)

- Verben mit Präposition behalten die **Präposition im Passivsatz,** z.B.

  Everybody laughed at him. (aktiv)
  He was laughed at by everybody. (passiv)

- **Passive Verlaufsformen** existieren nur für **Present** und **Past,** z.B.

  She is being asked. *They were being asked.*

- Passivformen werden vom Sprechenden gewählt, wenn der **Agierende unbekannt oder unwichtig** ist, oder **nicht erwähnt werden soll.** Auch kann der Sprechende seine Mitteilungsabsicht geschickt steuern: Im Passiv gelangt die **Information** in die bevorzugte **Endstellung** im Satz, z.B.

  I was bitten by a snake! (statt: *A snake bit me!*)

38 Exercises

I. Make these sentences sound more natural by changing them into passive forms. Only add a by-phrase where it is really necessary. ●●

1. A car ran over our pet cat last night.
2. Somebody shot a 23-year-old soldier in Londonderry.
3. A man is repairing my central heating today.
4. A child made this carpet in India.
5. You may not take photographs in this theatre.
6. Has somebody invited you to our party?
7. People speak English almost everywhere.
8. Someone has stolen my car!

II. Translate the sentences below into English beginning with the personal pronoun.

1. Man dankte ihr. (*She* …)
2. Uns wurde nichts versprochen. (*We* …)
3. Es wurde uns gesagt, wir sollten um neun Uhr kommen. (*We* …)
4. Man gab ihnen ein Geschenk.
5. Ihr wurde die Stadt gezeigt.
6. Man bat uns, einen kurzen Bericht zu schreiben.
7. Man hat uns zum Flughafen gebracht.
8. Ihnen wurde ein neues Kartenspiel beigebracht.

III. How many passive forms are there in this text? Why aren't there more? ●●

'I should like you to get me a ticket on the next flight to London,' she said, in a clear voice. 'And I should like to send a telegram.' When the requisite form had been found, she sat down at a small glass table in the lobby. 'Simmonds, Chiltern Street, London W1,' she wrote. 'Coming home.' But, after a moment, she thought that this was not entirely accurate and, crossing out the words 'Coming home,' wrote simply, 'Returning.'

(From *Hotel du Lac* by Anita Brookner)

39 Entsprechungen für ‚lassen‘ (Equivalents for ‚lassen‘)

Das deutsche Verb **‚lassen‘** hat mehrere Bedeutungen. Sie werden im Englischen durch unterschiedliche Verben ausgedrückt:

- Das Verb **‘to have sth done’** (*etw. machen lassen*) wird mit einer Form von **‘to have’ + Objekt + Partizip Perfekt** gebildet. ‘to have’ lässt als Vollverb alle Verbformen zu, z. B.

  We’re having our house painted. (Wir lassen unser Haus streichen.)
  He’s just had his hair cut. (Er ließ gerade erst sein Haar schneiden.)

  Die Konstruktion ‘to have sth done’ ist **von der Vorvergangenheit** (s. unit 31) **zu unterscheiden,** z. B.

  They had their car washed. (Sie ließen ihr Auto waschen.)
  They had washed their car. (Sie hatten ihr Auto gewaschen.)

- Das Verb **‘to make sb do sth’** (*jmdn. zu etw. veranlassen*) bereitet deshalb oft Schwierigkeiten, weil auf ‘somebody’ ein Infinitiv ***ohne*** **‘to’** folgt, z. B.

  He made us open our bags. (Er ließ uns unsere Taschen öffnen.)

- Das Verb **‘to let sb do sth’** (*jmdn. etw. machen lassen/jmdm. etw. erlauben*) führt ebenfalls den Infinitiv ***ohne*** **‘to’,** z. B.

  She let us go home early. (Sie ließ uns früh nach Hause gehen.)

- Feststehende idiomatische **Wendungen,** z. B.

Leave me alone!	(Lass mich in Ruhe!)
Give me time.	(Lass mir Zeit.)
Take your time.	(Lass dir Zeit.)

39 Exercises

I. Is it the 'have-something-done' structure or the past perfect simple? Mark the appropriate column.

	'have sth done'	past perfect simple
1. I've just had my eyes tested.		
2. We had seen it before.		
3. Have you had it repaired?		
4. Had you known that earlier?		
5. She's having the jacket cleaned.		
6. He had washed it before he returned it.		

II. Finish off these sentences using the 'have-something-done' structure. (Use the past participle of the verbs in the box below.) ●●

clean • cut • deliver • develop • paint • repair • send • take

1. Jill's coat is no longer dirty because she …
2. Theresa's hair is shorter now because she …
3. Malcolm's motorbike is working again now because he …
4. Geoff hasn't got his holiday photos with him because he …
5. Joe's wearing his smartest clothes because he … for a job application.
6. Warren doesn't go out and buy a paper every morning because he …
7. Mr Banks's old house looks much cleaner now because he …
8. Kate doesn't want to drive into town to pick up the tickets. She wants …

III. Rewrite the sentences using the 'have-something-done' structure. ●●

1. My father bought the television for us. *(We …)*
2. A friend of him records all the rugby matches for him. *(He …)*
3. Someone is repairing Anita's printer. *(Anita …)*
4. A gardener has cut Mrs Fleming's hedges (*Hecken*).
5. A professional photographer took Stephen and Clare's wedding photos.
6. The optician had tested Alison's eyes before she bought her new glasses.
7. A hairdresser always comes and cuts Penny's hair at home.
8. The box office has sent the tickets for the jazz concert to Charley's home address.

40 Zusammengesetzte Verben (Multi-word verbs)

Viele Verben im Englischen bestehen aus **zwei oder drei Teilen** wie 'to look at sth' (*etw. anschauen*), 'to get on with sb' (*mit jmdm. auskommen*) oder 'to turn down sth' (*etw. ablehnen*). Diese Verben werden **'multi-word verbs'** oder **'phrasal verbs'** genannt. Es gibt drei Arten:

1. Die **intransitiven** 'multi-word verbs' (d.h. **Verb + Partikel *ohne* direktes Objekt**) sind einfach in ihrer Struktur, weil **Verb und Partikel nicht trennbar** sind, z.B.

   How did that come about?
   They stayed up all night.

Bei den **transitiven** 'multi-word verbs' (d.h. **Verb + Partikel *mit* direktem Objekt**) muss man zwischen trennbaren und nicht trennbaren unterscheiden. Um festzustellen, ob transitive 'multi-word verbs' trennbar sind oder nicht, schlägt man in einem guten Wörterbuch nach.

2. Bei **trennbaren** transitiven 'multi-word verbs' kann das **Objekt zwischen Stammverb und Partikel, aber auch nach der Partikel** stehen, z.B.

   Can you blow the balloon up?
   Can you blow up the balloon?

   Wenn das Objekt des Verbs die Form eines **Pronomens** hat (d.h. 'it' statt 'balloon'), *muss* es **zwischen Verb und Partikel** stehen, z.B.

   Can you blow it up?

3. Bei **nicht trennbaren** transitiven 'multi-word verbs' folgt das **Objekt immer auf die Partikel,** z.B.

   The dog went for the postman.
   The dog went for him.

- Die **Bedeutung** der 'multi-word verbs' lässt sich vielfach aus den Einzelwörtern **ableiten,** z.B.

  Can I try on these shoes? ('try on' = anprobieren)

- Bei anderen 'multi-word verbs' gibt die Grundbedeutung der Einzelwörter ***keine* Auskunft** über die Bedeutung des Verbs, z.B.

  They can't get by on one salary. ('get by on' = zurechtkommen)

40 Exercises

I. Look at these idiomatic intransitive multi-word verbs. Match the verbs (1–8) to their 'meanings' (a–h). Then add a German translation for the verbs.

1. I'll drop in on the way home.	a. to have an argument
2. Don't wait up for me. I may be late.	b. to travel
3. Her work really stands out, doesn't it?	c. to fall asleep
4. He's fallen out with his girlfriend.	d. to get better
5. Dad's just dropped off.	e. to not go to bed
6. You get around a lot.	f. to visit for a short time
7. Things are looking up!	g. to put on one's best clothes
8. Do we have to dress up for the party?	h. to be of high quality

II. Write out the sentences below again using one of the multi-word verbs in the box instead of the verbs underlined. (Use a dictionary if you wish.) ●●

break off • dish out • give up • hold up • make up • set up • step up
wipe out

1. She ended the relationship.
2. He has stopped smoking.
3. We need to increase production.
4. I think you invented that story!
5. The explosion destroyed the village.
6. Can you distribute these leaflets to the houses in your street?
7. Do you know who organized this scheme by the way?
8. We were delayed in London because of the fog.

III. Link the multi-word verbs with their one-word equivalent. (Be careful. There are eight sentences and ten equivalents.)

	a. contact
1. They did away with the law.	b. support
2. Let's get down to business, shall we?	c. inform
3. She won't put up with behaviour like that.	d. abolish
4. It's OK. I'll stand in for you when you're away.	e. admire
5. Who's going to fill me in on the plan?	f. replace
6. Don't worry. We'll stick up for you!	g. succeed
7. You know he looks up to you, don't you?	h. tolerate
8. Leave it to me. I'll get on to them.	i. criticize
	j. start

41 Das Verb und seine Ergänzungen (Verb patterns)

Verben stehen selten alleine. Sie gehen **Verbindungen mit anderen Wörtern** ein, um komplexere Sätze zu bilden. Es gibt viele Möglichkeiten, Verben zu ergänzen, z. B.

Verb + 'that'-Satz, z. B.

She said that she was sorry.
We agreed that the holiday had been a success.
She suggested that they should meet a week later.
They hoped that they could visit us again.

Verb + Präposition (+ Gerund/Substantiv), z. B.

He dreams about becoming famous.
They apologized for being late.
She insisted on paying for the food.
I look forward to meeting you.

Verb + Infinitiv, z. B.

She managed to win.
They decided to agree.
I didn't want to say no.
He refused to stop smoking.

Verb + Substantiv/Gerund, z. B.

We enjoy dancing.
She admits being lazy.
You can't avoid making mistakes.
I don't mind working at night.

Verb + Objekt + Infinitiv (s. unit 48), z. B.

They warned us to stay at home.
We told him to ring again.
She reminded us to pay in advance.
He expected us to cooperate.

Verb + Objekt + Präposition, z. B.

They explained the problem to me.
We borrow books from the library.
She asked him for a lift.
I prefer tea to coffee.

Es ist wichtig, Verben stets zusammen mit ihren möglichen Ergänzungen zu lernen und dabei ein gutes einsprachiges Wörterbuch zu Rate zu ziehen. Die meisten Verben bieten eine ganze **Reihe von Ergänzungsmöglichkeiten,** z. B.

We hope that you're well.
She's hoping for a letter.
I hope to announce the winner shortly.

41 Exercises

I. Complete these sentences using the correct form of the verb in brackets. Add a preposition where necessary. ●●

1. I am thinking	
2. I am hoping	
3. I want	(get) a new job.
4. I might manage	
5. I don't mind	

II. Complete these sentences by using the correct form of the verb in brackets. Add a preposition where one is needed. ●●

1. I would like	
2. I think I'll succeed	
3. I have decided	(find) a well-paid job.
4. I hope	
5. I often dream	

III. Complete these sentences. Use the correct form of the verb in brackets. Add a preposition where one is required. ●●

1. I would refuse	
2. I will certainly avoid	
3. I wouldn't allow myself	(accept) a boring job.
4. I would prefer not	
5. I would hate	

IV. Read this extract from a novel. Use a dictionary. ●●

Work expands so as to fill the time available for its completion. Thus, an elderly lady of leisure can spend the entire day in writing and dispatching a postcard to her niece in Bognor Regis. An hour will be spent in finding the postcard, another in hunting for spectacles, half an hour in search for the address, an hour and a quarter in composition, and twenty minutes in deciding whether or not to take an umbrella when going to the pillar box in the next street.

(From *Parkinson's Law* by C. Northcote Parkinson)

42 If-Sätze (If-sentences)

Es gibt drei **Grundtypen** von If-Sätzen (Bedingungssätze):

TYP 1 **einfache Gegenwart** **'will' + Infinitiv**
If he gets the job, *I'll be very surprised.*
(d.h. es besteht eine reale Möglichkeit, dass er die Stelle bekommt)

TYP 2 **einfache Vergangenheit** **'would' + Infinitiv**
If he got the job, *I'd be very surprised.*
(d.h. es ist theoretisch möglich, aber unwahrscheinlich, dass er die Stelle bekommt)

TYP 3 **einfache Vorvergangenheit** **'would have' + Partizip Perfekt**
If he had got the job, *I would have been very surprised.*
(d.h. die Bedingung lässt sich nicht mehr erfüllen, weil die Stelle bereits besetzt ist)

- Der If-Satz kann **am Schluss des Satzes,** dann ohne Komma, stehen, z.B.

  I'd be very surprised if he got the job.

- Problematisch sind **If-Sätze nach Typ 2,** weil man als deutscher Muttersprachler dazu neigt, auch im If-Satzteil 'would' zu verwenden, z.B.

  We would lose our jobs if we went on strike.
  (Wir würden unsere Stellen verlieren, wenn wir streiken *würden.*)

- Es gibt If-Sätze, die andere als die o.g. Strukturen zulassen:
  In sog. **'zero if-sentences'** beispielsweise wird **keine Bedingung, sondern eine allgemein gültige Situation** zum Ausdruck gebracht. In diesem Fall steht in **beiden Satzhälften die einfache Form der Gegenwart,** z.B.

  Grass grows quickly if it rains a lot.

42 Exercises

I. Complete the sentences using the correct form of the words in brackets and type 1 if-clauses. (One sentence, however, contains a zero if-clause.) ●●

1. If you … (want) to see the show, I … (get) the tickets this afternoon.
2. If all … (go) well, … (we, be) there by this afternoon?
3. I … (sit) here if you … (not, mind).
4. We … (no, go running) this afternoon if it … (keep) raining.
5. How long … (milk, keep) if it … (not, be) in the fridge?
6. If they … (not, have) time, they … (not, be able) to come.

II. Complete the type 2 if-clause in these mini-dialogues. (You choose the verb!) ●●

1. How's my English?
   Great. I'd correct you if you … a mistake.
2. Where are we exactly?
   I've no idea. It'd be helpful if we … a map.
3. Shall we take a taxi?
   Wouldn't it be cheaper if we … by bus?
4. She's French, isn't she?
   It'd be good if we … some French.
5. Can you look after our dog while we're away next week?
   If we … here, I would. But we're also away.

III. Use type 3 if-clauses to complete the following sentences. ●●

1. If he … (tell) us he was coming, we … (certainly, wait) for him.
2. I … (come round) and … (see) you if I … (have) the time.
3. They … (lend) their son some money to buy a car if he … (save) more of his own.
4. If she … (be) a bit more careful, she … (not, have) the accident.
5. If the train … (not, be) late, he … (probably, get to) work on time.
6. I … (help) you if you … (ask) me.

IV. Is the 'd the short form for 'had' or 'would'?
Put a mark in the appropriate box.

1. You'd better come and see what's happened.
2. I'd have rung you! Really!
3. If we'd had the time, we would have called in.
4. I'd like a single room with bath.

'had'	'would'

43 'I wish ...'

- Auf 'I wish' folgen oft **'would' oder 'could' + Infinitiv ohne 'to'.** Diese Form drückt die Unzufriedenheit mit einer Situation aus, den Wunsch, dass etw. passiert oder jmd. etw. unternimmt, z. B.

  I wish I could get another job.
  (Ich wünschte, ich könnte eine andere Stelle bekommen.)

- 'I wish' wird auch in Verbindung mit **Vergangenheitsformen** verwendet. Ähnlich wie bei If-Sätzen (s. unit 42), beschreibt das Tempus der Vergangenheit eine **gegenwärtige Situation.** Der geäußerte Wunsch ist theoretisch erfüllbar, dem Sprechenden erscheint seine Realisierung jedoch **unwahrscheinlich,** z. B.

  I wish I knew the answer.
  (Ich wünschte, ich wüsste die Antwort.)

- Nach 'I wish' kann auch eine **Vorvergangenheitsform** stehen. Hier lässt sich der Wunsch des Sprechenden selbst theoretisch **nicht mehr erfüllen,** weil die **Situation in der Vergangenheit** liegt, z. B.

  I wish I had had the chance to speak to him before he died.
  (Ich wünschte, ich hätte die Gelegenheit gehabt, mit ihm zu sprechen, bevor er starb.)

43 Exercises

I. What do you say? Read the situation and think of a sentence beginning with 'I wish ...'.

1. You want to go out for a walk but it keeps raining.
2. The telephone is ringing and nobody is answering it.
3. You're trying to sleep and your neighbours are playing loud music.
4. You're sitting in your friend's car and he is driving very dangerously.
5. You've been waiting over half an hour for a taxi but it still hasn't come.
6. You're expecting your girlfriend/boyfriend to call you but she/he hasn't yet.

II. Write a sentence beginning with 'I wish ...' which describes a present situation. (You may have to add some of your own words.) ●●

1. I don't have many friends – but I'd like to.
2. I don't drive my own car – but I'd like to.
3. I don't earn enough money – but I'd like to.
4. I don't live in the city – but I'd like to.
5. I don't look very fit – but I'd like to.
6. I don't know enough English words – but I'd like to.

III. The sentences below describe past situations. Add a sentence beginning with 'I wish ...'. (As before, you may have to add some of your own words.) ●●

1. It's a shame I didn't know him very well.
2. It's a pity that we didn't have a warmer summer.
3. It's a pity I didn't get on well with my brothers.
4. It's a shame that I didn't take a holiday last year.
5. It's a pity that we were not at home when they called.
6. It's a shame they didn't invite us to the wedding.

44 Indirekte Rede I (Indirect speech I)

In der indirekten Rede wird **berichtet, wovon jemand gesprochen hat,** ohne den genauen Wortlaut wiederzugeben.

- Steht das **einleitende Verb in der einfachen Vergangenheit,** werden in der indirekten Rede oft **andere Zeitformen** verwendet.

Zeitverschiebung:

Present → **Past**	*'**I'm** tired,' said Rick.* *Rick said (that) he **was** tired.* *'**I'm looking** for a good book,' said Pam.* *Pam said (that) she **was looking** for a good book.*
Past → **Past Perfect**	*'I **met** Jane in the butcher's,' said Brenda.* *Brenda said (that) she **had met** Jane in the butcher's.* *'I **was driving** along the High Street when I saw Pia,' said Dick.* *Dick said (that) he **had been driving** along the High Street when he had seen Pia.*
Present Perfect → **Past Perfect**	*'**I've** never **been** to London,' said Tania.* *Tania said (that) she **had** never **been** to London.* *'**I've been waiting** all morning for your call,' said Ed.* *Ed said (that) he **had been waiting** all morning for my call.*
Future 'will' → **Conditional 'would'**	*'**I'll pick** you **up** tomorrow, Terry,' said Anna.* *Anna said (that) she **would pick** Terry **up** the day after.*
Future 'will have' → **Conditional 'would have'**	*'**I'll have picked** you up by ten tomorrow,' said she.* *She said (that) she**'d have picked** her up by ten the following day.*

- Wichtige Verben, die neben 'say' die **indirekte Rede einleiten** können: 'to add' (*hinzufügen*), 'to claim' (*behaupten*), 'to explain' (*erklären*), 'to report' (*berichten*), 'to reply' (*erwidern*)

44 Exercises

I. You meet a friend of yours, Martin, in a café. He tells you a lot of things. Later you speak to Malcolm. Use the rules of reported speech to tell Malcolm what Martin told you. ●●

Martin said:

1. 'My sister has a new boyfriend.' (*He said that his sister …*)
2. 'I've bought a new mountain bike.'
3. 'I don't know where Joe is living.'
4. 'I'm going to Rachel's wedding on Saturday.'
5. 'I've been trying to get fit recently.'
6. 'We can go out together on Friday night.'
7. 'My father has retired.'
8. 'My job is getting so boring.'

II. Complete these sentences with 'said', 'told' or 'talked'. ●●

1. Paul … me he had found a new job.
2. Martha … she couldn't come to the meeting.
3. Ann … Mike to go home.
4. George … about his holiday all evening.
5. Josh … that he's got a new flat.
6. Steve … and the others just listened.
7. Bob … the truth. But was it the whole truth?
8. Kate … us she had to go into hospital.

III. Report these words and thoughts by starting with the verb given. You may have to add some words. ●●

1. 'I'm leaving Germany tomorrow,' Richard told us.
   Richard said …
2. 'You're crazy!' Donna said to Ray. 'It just won't work!'
   Donna told …
3. 'Anna has paid for the meal,' Celia told Catherine.
   Catherine was told …
4. 'Dinner is served between seven and ten,' said the receptionist.
   The receptionist explained …
5. 'It took me an hour longer than usual to get here, ' Jason said.
   Jason explained …

45 Indirekte Rede II (Indirect speech II)

- Auch bei **indirekten Fragesätzen** findet i.d.R. eine **Zeitverschiebung** statt. Das Fragewort des Aussagesatzes bleibt; das Subjekt steht vor dem Verb. Ist kein Fragewort vorhanden, wird der indirekte Fragesatz mit 'if' (*ob, wenn*) oder 'whether' (*ob*) eingeleitet. Das Fragezeichen entfällt, z.B.

  'When did you get home?' he asked.
  He asked when she had got home.

  'Did you get home?' he asked.
  He asked if/whether she had got home.

- Bei **Aufforderungen** und **Bitten** wird die indirekte Rede durch die Konstruktion **Verb + Objekt + Infinitiv mit 'to'** wiedergegeben (s. unit 48), z.B.

  'Sit down please, Mrs Banks,' he said.
  He asked Mrs Banks to sit down.

- **Kommas** und **Anführungszeichen entfallen** in der indirekten Rede. **Pronomen, Orts- und Zeitangaben** müssen i.d.R. **verändert** werden, z.B.

I	→	***he, she***
we	→	***they***
here	→	***there***
this, these	→	***that, those***
yesterday	→	***the day before, the previous day***
tomorrow	→	***the day after, the following day***
ago, last	→	***before***

45 Exercises

I. Which sentences below (a–d) report the question above? There is more than one answer in each group.

1. *The man said, 'What's your number, Sarah?'*

a. He asked her what was her number.
b. He asked her what her number was.
c. He asked what her number was.
d. He wanted to know her number.

2. *'Do you like it, John?' he asked.*

a. He asked him whether he liked it or not.
b. He asked him if he liked it.
c. He asked if he likes.
d. He asked do you like?

3. *'What are you looking at, Joe?' I asked.*

a. I wanted to know what he was looking at.
b. I didn't know what he was looking at.
c. I wondered what he was looking at.
d. I thought what was he looking at.

II. Rewrite these sentences in different ways. Change the meaning as little as possible. Start in the way shown. ●●

1. 'Take the job, Clive!' Sally said.	a. Sally suggested that … b. Sally advised …
2. 'Kevin should really study,' the teacher said.	a. The teacher recommended … b. The teacher wanted …
3. 'Give me the documents, David,' his boss said.	a. The boss asked … b. The boss ordered …
4. 'Visit us whenever you can,' Sue's father said.	a. Her father expected … b. Her father insisted …

III. Change these sentences into indirect speech. Remember to make all the small changes which are necessary. ●●

1. 'Were you here yesterday, Jane?' he asked.
2. 'Are you coming tomorrow, Paul?' she asked.
3. 'I was here two hours ago!' she said.
4. 'I love you, Johanna,' he said.

46 Relativsätze (Relative clauses)

Ein Relativsatz **beschreibt ein Substantiv näher.** Im folgenden Satz etwa wird das Substantiv 'man' durch den Relativsatz 'who works in the post office' näher bestimmt, z. B.

The man who works in the post office is my uncle.

- Es gibt **zwei Arten** von Relativsätzen:

  1. Relativsätze, die für das Verständnis des ganzen Satzes notwendig sind, weil sie die **entscheidende Information** liefern, nennt man **bestimmend** ('defining'). Sie werden **ohne Kommas** geschrieben, z. B.

  The computer which we've just bought was not too expensive.

  2. Nicht bestimmende ('non-defining') Relativsätze stehen zwischen **Kommas** und **können ausgeklammert werden,** ohne den Sinn des ganzen Satzes zu entstellen, z. B.

  Her father, who was a famous actor, was very rarely at home.

- Nur bei **bestimmenden** Relativsätzen können die **Relativpronomen** 'that', 'who' und 'which' als Objekt des Relativsatzes (s. unit 9) **entfallen,** z. B.

  Have you seen the dog (–) they've got?

46 Exercises

I. Are these relative clauses defining or non-defining? Put a mark in the correct column.

	Def.	Non-def.
1. London, which lies on the Thames, is the British capital.		
2. The city in Britain I like most is Glasgow.		
3. The people I spoke to were really friendly.		
4. My mother, who lives nearby, often looks after our children.		
5. The island off the British south coast is called the Isle of Wight.		
6. The Canary Islands, which are popular with tourists, lie nearer to France than Britain.		

II. Join the two sentences into one by using a relative clause. The first part of each sentence has been done for you. ●●

1. Craig is wearing a new jacket. Rick likes it.
   Rick likes the new jacket …
2. Kim's parents stayed in a hotel in Portugal. It wasn't too expensive.
   The hotel in Portugal …
3. The milk was sour. We were served it for breakfast.
   The milk …
4. Amanda understands me. She's the only person who does.
   Amanda …
5. Trevor went to a disco. It was very loud and overcrowded.
   The disco …
6. Lucy has applied for a job. It's in Sweden.
   The job …
7. The concert was sold out. We wanted tickets for it.
   The concert …
8. A young girl answered the phone. She told me you were at work.
   The young girl …

III. Read this extract from a novel. ●●

Frances lay back in her aeroplane seat, and closed her eyes. The woman next to her, who was going out to Spain to spend Christmas with her son who had married a girl from Seville, was very anxious to be conversational (… *auf ein Gespräch aus*), so Frances had to say, gently and untruthfully, 'I'm so sorry, I've got a wicked (*böse*) headache. I'm just going to close my eyes.'

(From *A Spanish Lover* by Joanna Trollope)

47 Das Gerund (The gerund)

- Das Gerund ist gleich der **-ing-Form** des Verbs. Es kann **Subjekt wie Objekt** eines Satzes sein, z.B.

Flying is faster than going by train. *We love walking.*
Smoking is bad for your health. *She enjoys cycling.*

- **Verben,** nach denen das Gerund steht:

avoid	***enjoy***	***mind***	***practise***
deny	***give up***	***miss***	***resist***
dislike	***imagine***	***postpone***	***suggest***

- Das Gerund ist die **einzig mögliche Verbform nach einer Präposition,** ob Verb + Präposition, Adjektiv + Präposition, Substantiv + Präposition oder allein stehende Präposition, z.B.

*They **object to** sitting in a dark room.*
*He **insists on** wearing a tie.*
*I'm **looking forward to** meeting you.*
***Thank** you **for** being so helpful.*
*Are you **fond of** listening to music?*
*She used to be **good at** playing cards.*
*Do you ever get **tired of** teaching?*
*We had **difficulty in** making ourselves clear.*
*There's a **danger of** losing a lot of money.*
*I have great **pleasure in** introducing Mrs Brown.*
***Instead of** saying sorry he laughed.*
*He left the room **without** saying goodbye.*

- Wichtige **Ausdrücke,** auf die das Gerund folgt:

It's no use …	(Es hat keinen Zweck ...)
It's good fun …	(Es macht Spaß ...)
It's bad enough …	(Es ist schlimm genug ...)
I don't mind …	(Es macht mir nichts aus ...)
I can't stand …	(Ich hasse ...)
There's no point …	(Es ist sinnlos ...)
It's worth ...	(Es lohnt sich ...)

47 Exercises

I. Complete these sentences using the gerund. Which gerunds are subjects of the verb and which are objects? ●●

1. (travel) abroad can be very inspiring.
2. Is (cheat) in an exam unfair in your opinion?
3. (Have) to listen to loud music can be very annoying.
4. Do you like (ski) or do you prefer (ice-skate)?
5. Would you mind (answer) the phone?
6. Imagine (live) in a place where there's no electricity.
7. The children enjoy (walk) - as long as it's not too far.
8. Did she avoid (talk) or even (look) at us?

II. To complete these sentences you need to add the correct preposition and the gerund form of the verb in brackets. (Use a dictionary if you wish.) ●●

1. He apologized … (be) late.
2. He's fond … (read) but even more keen … (watch) TV.
3. She was blamed … (ruin) the evening.
4. They're thinking … (emigrate) to South Africa.
5. Have you ever dreamt … (be) a sports star?
6. He had no intention … (hurt) her feelings.
7. She's good … (play) the violin and even better … (perform) on stage.
8. Congratulations … (do) so well in your exams!

III. Read this extract from a novel. ●●

I don't know why it matters so much. Ian could be better at talking than me, or cooking, or working, or housework, or saving money, or earning money, or spending money, or understanding books or films, he could be nicer than me, better-looking, more intelligent, cleaner, more generous-spirited, more helpful, a better human being in any way you care to mention … and I wouldn't mind. Really. I accept and understand that you can't be good at everything, and I am tragically unskilled in some very important areas. But sex is different; knowing that a successor (*Nachfolger*) is better in bed is impossible to take, and I don't know why.

(From *High Fidelity* by Nick Hornby)

48 Der Infinitiv (The infinitive)

Der Infinitiv (z. B. 'to go') ist die Grundform des Verbs und sagt nichts aus über Person, Zahl oder Zeit. Es gibt zwei Arten: den Infinitiv **mit und ohne 'to':**

- Der **Infinitv ohne 'to'** folgt auf die **modalen Hilfsverben** (s. units 15ff.), z. B.

  I can't hear you.

  Andere Verben und Konstruktionen mit Infinitiv ohne 'to' (s. unit 21 u. 39), z. B.

*They didn't **dare** say a word.*	*You'**d better** go.*
*You **need**n't worry.*	*She **made** me pay.*
*I'**d rather** work here.*	*He **let** me suffer.*

- Der **Infinitiv mit 'to'** folgt auf viele Verben, Adjektive und Substantive, z. B.

  What do you want to see?
  Where would you like to go?
  They decided to have a holiday.
  I hope to come back soon.
  They promised to tell the truth.
  I am surprised to see you here.
  It's difficult to understand.
  She's happy to earn her own money.
  Was it her decision to marry him?
  He ignored her wish to be alone.

- Der **Infinitiv mit 'to'** kann **Nebensätze verkürzen,** z. B.

  I don't know what to do. (statt: *I don't know what I should do.*)
  Can you tell me when to speak? (statt: ... *when I should speak?*)

  Mit der Konstruktion **'for' + Substantiv/Pronomen + Infinitiv mit 'to'** lassen sich **'if'-** und **'that'-Sätze ersetzen,** z. B.

  Is it possible for us to get cheaper tickets?
  It's perfectly all right for you to stay with us at the weekend.

  Die im Deutschen seltenere Satzkonstruktion **Verb + Objekt + Infinitiv mit 'to'** kann ebenfalls **Nebensätze vermeiden** helfen, z. B.

  She expects him to call. (Sie erwartet, dass er anruft.)
  Remind me to buy some milk. (Erinnere mich, Milch zu kaufen.)

I'd **like**	**you**	**to stay**.
V	**O**	**I**

Weitere Verben, bei denen **kein 'that'-Satz** möglich ist:

to advise sb + inf.	***to encourage sb*** + inf.	***to persuade sb*** + inf.
to allow sb + inf.	***to invite sb*** + inf.	***to rely on sb*** + inf.
to ask sb + inf.	***to like sb*** + inf.	***to teach sb*** + inf.
to count on sb + inf.	***to order sb*** + inf.	***to tell sb*** + inf.

48 Exercises

I. Complete the sentences using the correct form of the words in brackets and an infinitive construction with or without 'to'. ●●

1. He (would like, have) his own car but he can't really afford one.
2. She (not, dare, laugh) when her teacher fell off his bike outside the school.
3. It wasn't our (decision, go) on foot. It was yours!
4. You (not, must, leave) your car here. It's somebody else's parking space.
5. I (not, be able, get) tickets because it's already sold out.
6. We're (too old, go) to discos, parties and things like that.
7. They (decide, wait) until the next morning before watering the garden.
8. It's (dangerous, play) here because of all the traffic.

II. Translate the following sentences using an infinitive construction. ●●

1. Können Sie mir bitte sagen, wo ich parken soll?
2. Wir wissen wirklich nicht, welches Buch wir nehmen sollen.
3. Weißt du, wo man mehr über britische Universitäten erfahren (*find out*) kann?
4. Es ist warm genug, um draußen essen zu können.
5. Das Beste (*best thing*) wäre, wenn ich eine Stelle fände.
6. Der Tee ist zu stark, als dass ich ihn trinken könnte.

III. Use the correct form of the words in brackets to form complete sentences. ●●

1. Would you like (I, help) you?
2. They asked (she, think) about her future in the company.
3. We managed to persuade (he, not, go).
4. Could you tell (they, hurry up), please!
5. We would like to invite (you, have) dinner with us some time.
6. They advised (he, finish) his studies before starting a family.
7. Who taught (she, drive)?
8. They have arranged for (we, borrow) their car for a week.

49 Gerund oder Infinitiv (Gerund or infinitive)

- Es gibt Verben, Substantive und Adjektive, die ohne Bedeutungsverschiebung **sowohl mit Gerund als auch mit Infinitiv** verwendet werden können, z.B.

  More and more people like working (to work) from home.
  We prefer having (to have) a holiday in the winter than the summer.
  They intend going (to go) to the States for a year.
  Is there a quick way of learning (to learn) a foreign language?
  She's not afraid of defending (to defend) her opinions.

- Die Verben **'to stop', 'to remember'** und **'to forget'** haben **unterschiedliche Bedeutung,** je nach Gebrauch von Gerund oder Infinitiv. Die Konstruktion mit Gerund hat **rückblickenden,** diejenige mit Infinitiv **vorausschauenden** Charakter, z.B.

He stopped drinking.	(aufhören, etw. zu tun)
He stopped to drink.	(aufhören, um etw. zu tun)
I can remember filming them.	(s. erinnern, etw. getan zu haben)
Please remember to phone her.	(daran denken, etw. zu tun)
She won't forget passing her exams.	(vergessen, etw. getan zu haben)
She didn't forget to post the letter.	(vergessen, etw. zu tun)

- Auf das Vollverb **'to be used to'** folgt **Gerund (oder Substantiv),** z.B.

I am used to getting up early.	(Ich bin es gewöhnt, früh aufzustehen.)

- Auf **'used to'** folgt stets **Infinitiv,** z.B.

I used to listen to a lot of music.	(Früher hörte ich viel Musik.)

- Auf **Verben der Sinneswahrnehmung,** wie 'to hear', 'to notice', 'to see' und 'to watch', folgt **Objekt + Infinitiv ohne 'to'** oder **Gerund.** Der Infinitiv drückt aus, dass die **Handlung als Ganzes** gesehen wird; die -ing-Form betont, dass die **Handlung gerade im Gange** ist, z.B.

  We saw the child run over the road.
  (Wir sahen das Kind über die Straße laufen.)
  We saw the child running over the road.
  (Wir sahen, wie das Kind über die Straße lief.)

49 Exercises

I. To complete four of these sentences you can use a preposition + gerund or an infinitive + 'to'. In one sentence, however, you must use a preposition + gerund. ●●

1. She is (keen, do) well at school.
2. We're not (afraid, make) mistakes. Are you?
3. What's the best (way, find) a holiday job?
4. Thank you (be) so understanding.
5. Is there a (chance, leave) a bit earlier?

II. Which sentences describe a past action? Which describe something in the present? Mark the appropriate column.

	past	present
1. He used to work for an American pharmaceutical company.		
2. She was used to speaking English in her job.		
3. They're used to having people in their house.		
4. I didn't use to like him.		
5. We used to live in a tiny village.		
6. She never used to get angry so quickly.		

III. Identify the appropriate end of the sentence. ●●

1. He stopped smoking …	a. and his health began to improve.
2. He stopped to smoke …	b. and then carried on.
3. Remember to go to the bank …	a. when Uncle Alex worked there?
4. Do you remember going to the bank …	b. and find out about exchange rates.
5. I'll always forget to write to her …	a. when I didn't know much English.
6. I'll never forget writing to her in LA …	b. because she never writes to me.

IV. One of these sentences sounds strange to an English ear. Which one is it and why?

1. I saw something fall.
2. I smelt something burn.
3. I noticed something move.

50 Das Partizip Präsens (The present participle)

Das Partizip Präsens (Mittelwort der Gegenwart) **endet auf -ing.**

- Das Partizip Präsens kann als **Adjektiv** verwendet werden, z. B.

  Let sleeping dogs lie. (Schlafende Hunde weckt man nicht.)

- Das Partizip Präsens verbindet oft **gleichzeitige Handlungen,** z. B.

  She lay in bed reading the paper. (Sie lag im Bett und las Zeitung.)
  'Bye,' he said, smiling. (‚Wiedersehen', sagte er, lächelnd.)

- Das Partizip Präsens kann einen **Relativsatz,** der ein Vollverb in aktiver, d. h. nicht passiver Form enthält, **verkürzen,** z. B.

  The man standing (statt: *who is standing) over there looks like you.*
  The train arriving (statt: *which is arriving) at ten is going to Reading.*

  Auch **Temporalsätze** in aktiver Form können mit dem Partizip Präsens **verkürzt** werden, z. B.

  After arriving (statt: *After they had arrived) at Heathrow, they took a taxi to central London.*
  Before leaving (statt: *Before she leaves) home, she always checks that all the windows are closed.*

  Bei **Kausalsätzen** in aktiver Form **ersetzt** das Partizip Präsens die **Konjunktionen** 'as', 'because', 'since' etc., z. B.

  Having (statt: *As we had) little money to spare, we slept out in the open.*
  Knowing (statt: *Since I knew) what I knew, I had to tell them the story.*

  Auch aktive **Konzessivsätze** können mit dem Partizip Präsens **verkürzt** werden. Die Konjunktion bleibt, z. B.

  Although being poor (statt: *Although she was poor), she kept her dignity.*

Die **Konjunktionen**	in Kausalsätzen	**müssen immer**	weggelassen (werden).
	in Temporalsätzen	**werden oft**	
	in Konzessivsätzen	**dürfen nie**	

50 Exercises

I. Join the two sentences together using a participle construction. ●●

1. I got home. I felt tired.
2. The man sat on the park bench. He was talking to himself.
3. He cut himself. He was peeling onions.
4. 'Is this seat free?' he asked and pointed to a chair next to her.
5. They were in London. They were visiting their daughter.
6. I often spend the evening at home. I listen to music or read.
7. She came into the room. She looked around and smiled.
8. He ran into the house. He was shouting and waving his arms.

II. Use a participle construction to shorten the relative clause. ●●

1. Who is the old woman who lives opposite you?
2. I'd like to get a job which can offer better career opportunities.
3. Do you know about the problems which are facing the environment?
4. Identify the sentences which contain a participle construction.
5. Did you see that car which drove over the red lights?
6. Although she was ill, she went to work.

III. Lengthen these sentences by using a full relative clause. ●●

1. The train arriving at platform 5 is the 10.15 from Bristol Parkway.
2. People travelling to work on the M25 should expect delays.
3. They were given a room overlooking Hyde Park.
4. Models reaching the top of their profession can earn a lot of money.
5. Did you see that man outside the bank holding a big suitcase?

IV. Do these present participles express a time for doing something or give a reason for something? Mark the appropriate column.

	Time	Reason
1. Having lost his job, he was very unhappy.		
2. Knowing my brother, I never lend him any money.		
3. Not wanting to be late, I decided to cycle and not walk.		
4. Taking a key out of his pocket, he quietly opened the door.		

V. Translate these sentences into German bringing out the difference in meaning.

1. Being late for her interview, Kate didn't have time for breakfast.
2. Being late for an interview is very annoying.

51 Das Partizip Perfekt (The past participle)

Das Partizip Perfekt (Mittelwort der Vergangenheit) **endet auf -ed,** bildet allerdings viele **unregelmäßige Formen** (s. S. 133ff.).

- Das Partizip Perfekt kann als **Adjektiv** verwendet werden, z. B.

  The stolen car was found in an underground car park.

- Das Partizip Perfekt kann einen **Relativsatz** mit einem Vollverb im Passiv **verkürzen,** z. B.

  The number of people killed (statt: *who are killed) in road accidents is increasing.*
  Most books written (statt: *which are written) by football stars are extremely boring.*

  Auch **Temporalsätze** im Passiv können mit dem Partizip Perfekt **verkürzt** werden. Wird ein Satz mit 'after' oder 'before' eingeleitet, wird i. d. R. der Zusatz **'being'** verlangt, z. B.

  After being told (statt: *After they had been told) to leave the pub, the youths began to shout aggressively.*
  Before being shown (statt: *Before he was shown) to the interview room, John had to fill in a form.*

  Bei **Kausalsätzen** im Passiv **ersetzt** das Partizip Perfekt die entsprechende **Konjunktion** ('as', 'because', 'since'), z. B.

  Surprised (statt: *As she had been surprised) by her father's comment, Gillian didn't know what to say next.*
  Warned (statt: *Since he had been warned) to be careful at night in NY, William took a cab to his hotel.*

  Auch passive **Konzessivsätze** können mit Partizip Perfekt **verkürzt** werden, wobei die Konjunktion ('although') nie entfallen darf, z. B.

  Although (he was) hit by a stroke of bad luck, he remained confident.

Verkürzte Relativsätze sind **typisch** für das gesprochene wie geschriebene Englisch. Verkürzte Temporal-, Kausal- und Konzessivsätze gehören eher der formalen Schriftsprache an.

51 Exercises

I. Shorten the relative clauses by using a participle construction. ●●

1. Books which are borrowed from the library must be returned within two weeks.
2. Toni Morrison's first book, which was written in 1970, was *The Bluest Eye*.
3. Some animals which are hunted for their skins will soon be extinct.
4. The advice which was given to him was simple: eat less, exercise more.
5. The jobs which were offered to me were all badly paid.

II. Lengthen the sentences by using a full relative clause. ●●

1. Most of the clothes sold here are made in Portugal.
2. All letters posted before five o'clock should reach their destination by the following morning.
3. The people injured in the accident have been released from hospital.
4. The houses built in this part of town will have to be pulled down.
5. The window broken in yesterday's storm has been repaired.

III. Join the half-sentences together. ●●

1. Before being given the sack	a. she decided to end their relationship.
2. Brought up in Oregon	b. the two men gave a party for their friends.
3. After being warned of the danger	c. the passengers' passports were inspected.
4. Hurt by her boyfriend's remarks	d. nobody let the children swim in the sea.
5. Before being asked to board	e. he spoke English with an American accent.
6. Congratulated on their success	f. he was asked to explain his behaviour.

IV. Read this extract from a novel. ●●

When he started out that morning from his home in Lancashire, he had had two packets of sandwiches in his pockets, made the night before by his mother. The egg sandwiches were wrapped in white paper and the ham in brown; they were each tied firmly, but not tightly, with string. But at a quarter to one he was sitting in a full compartment (*Abteil*), with no prospect of changing for fifty minutes and as he was shy of eating in front of strangers he looked anxiously at the other passengers to see if they were going to produce food themselves. They did not look as if they were.

(From *Jill* by Philip Larkin)

52 Nebensätze (Subclauses)

Ein Hauptsatz ('main clause') kann allein stehen. Ein Nebensatz ('subclause') dagegen ist von einem **Hauptsatz abhängig.** Einen Satz, bestehend aus Hauptsatz und einem oder mehreren Nebensätzen, nennt man Satzgefüge ('complex sentence'). Viele Nebensätze werden durch **Konjunktionen eingeleitet.**

- **Nebensätze der Zeit** (Temporalsätze, 'time clauses') werden durch Konjunktionen wie 'after', 'before', 'since', 'when', 'as soon as' (*sobald*) und 'while' (*während*) eingeleitet, z. B.

  What have you been doing since we last met?

  Auch wenn sich das Verb eines Nebensatzes der Zeit auf die **Zukunft** bezieht, steht es in der **einfachen Form der Gegenwart,** ohne 'will'/'shall' oder 'would'/'should', z. B.

  As soon as I get my results, I'll phone you.

- **Nebensätze des Grundes** (Kausalsätze, 'reason clauses') werden durch 'because', 'as' (*da*), 'due to' (*aufgrund*), 'in view of' (*angesichts*) oder 'since' (*da*) eingeleitet, z. B.

  She can't come because she has to study for her exams.

- Konjunktionen wie 'to' (*um … zu*), 'in order to' (*um … zu*), 'so that' (*damit*) und 'in order that' (*damit*) leiten **Nebensätze des Zwecks** (Finalsätze, 'purpose clauses') ein, z. B.

  We ran as fast as we could to catch the train.

- **Einräumungssätze** (Konzessivsätze, 'concession clauses') werden durch 'although', 'even though' (*obwohl*) oder 'whatever' (*was auch immer*) eingeleitet, z. B.

  Although he's quite young, he's got a lot of experience.

- Auch **If-** und **Relativsätze** (s. units 42 u. 46) sind Nebensätze, weil sie Hauptsätzen untergeordnet sind.

52 Exercises

I. Choose one of the conjunctions in the brackets to form an appropriate sentence.

1. My sister got married (after/until/when) university.
2. Did you see me (whenever/before/while) I was cycling along the High Street?
3. (After/Until/When) you go to England, you must spend some time in Cornwall.
4. Please ring us (after/as soon as/while) you can. We want to know exactly what happened!

II. Link the half-sentences together. (There are fewer first halves than second!) ●●

1. Since they haven't got any money,
2. As she's just had a baby,
3. Due to the bad weather,
4. The trains aren't running

a. the match has been cancelled.
b. she can't work as much as before.
c. the clocks have stopped.
d. because of the strike.
e. they can't go on holiday this year.
f. the weather has turned much colder.

III. Which word is missing? Is it 'although' or 'because'?

1. She flew … she had to get to the meeting early.
2. She flew … air fares are very expensive.
3. He decided to book a holiday in Florida … the weather at home had been so nice.
4. He decided to book a holiday in Florida … the weather at home had been so bad.

IV. Complete the following sentences using the correct form of the word in brackets. ●●

1. You shouldn't go back to work until your cold (get) better.
2. I'll tell you everything as soon as I (be) back at home.
3. You'll know who the murderer is when you (see) the second part.
4. We want to buy a house before they (go) up in price.

53 Amerikanisches Englisch (American English)

- Im amerikanischen Englisch wird in Verbindung mit **'just', 'already'** und **'yet'** i.d.R. **Past Simple** als Vergangenheitsform benutzt; im britischen Englisch wird üblicherweise **Present Perfect Simple** verwendet (s. unit 29), z.B.

They just went home. (AE)	*They've just gone home.* (BE)

- Im amerikanischen Englisch wird das Vollverb **'to have'** benutzt. Im britischen Englisch wird **'have got'** bevorzugt (s. unit 22), z.B.

She has two kids. (AE)	*She's got two children.* (BE)

- Im amerikanischen Englisch wird gelegentlich der **bestimmte Artikel,** im Gegensatz zum britischen Englisch, weggelassen, z.B.

He plays piano. (AE)	*He plays the piano.* (BE)

- Im amerikanischen Englisch, v.a. in der Umgangsprache, entfällt manchmal die **-ly-Endung** bei bestimmten Adjektiven und Adverbien, z.B.

She speaks real quick. (AE)	*She speaks really quickly.* (BE)

- Im amerikanischen Englisch ist die **Rechtschreibung** in vielen Fällen anders als im britischen Englisch, z.B.

color	*colour*
tire	*tyre*
theater	*theatre*
gray	*grey*
to practice (AE)	*to practise* (BE)

- Im amerikanischen Englisch werden manchmal andere **Präpositionen** verwendet als im britischen Englisch, z.B.

on the weekend	*at the weekend*
on a team	*in a team*
a quarter after three (AE)	*a quarter past three* (BE)

- Amerikanisches und britisches Englisch unterscheiden sich oft im Gebrauch des **Wortschatzes,** z.B.

elevator	*lift*
gas	*petrol*
subway (AE)	*underground* (BE)

53 Exercises

I. Write these sentences in American English. ●●

1. He's just gone home.
2. Has she spoken to you yet?
3. Have you got a problem?
4. Shall we meet at twenty past two?
5. What will the weather be like at the weekend?

II. Write these words with American spelling. Use a dictionary if you want.

1. litre	4. defence
2. favour	5. whisky
3. cheque	6. to analyse

III. Complete the sentences below using the correct words from the box. ●●

candy • downtown • elevator • fall • fries • garbage • gas • sidewalk store • vacation

1. We need some more … . The tank's nearly empty.
2. I like …, when the leaves turn red and yellow.
3. Do you want some … with your cheeseburger?
4. Our apartment's on the top floor so we'll take the … .
5. You shouldn't eat so much … . It's bad for your teeth.
6. Don't park your car on the …! You'll get a ticket.
7. How much … do you get in the States? Four weeks?
8. It smells bad in here! Is it your …?
9. We like city life. That's why we have an apartment in the … area.
10. Is there a … near here where I can get a paper?

IV. Read this extract from a novel. ●●

Robert Jordan lay behind the trunk (*Stamm*) of a pine tree on the slope (*Abhang*) of the hill above the road and the bridge and watched it become daylight. He loved this hour of the day always and now he watched it; feeling it gray within him, as though he were a part of the slow lightening that comes before the rising of the sun; when solid things darken and space lightens and the lights that have shone in the night go yellow and they fade as the day comes.

(From *For Whom the Bell Tolls* by Ernest Hemingway)

54 Zahlen (Numbers)

Grundzahlen:

0 nought/zero/'oh'	*11 eleven*	*30 thirty*
1 one	*12 twelve*	*40 forty*
2 two	*13 thirteen*	*50 fifty*
3 three	*14 fourteen*	*60 sixty*
4 four	*15 fifteen*	*70 seventy*
5 five	*16 sixteen*	*80 eighty*
6 six	*17 seventeen*	*90 ninety*
7 seven	*18 eighteen*	*100 a hundred*
8 eight	*19 nineteen*	*200 two hundred*
9 nine	*20 twenty*	*1,000 a thousand*
10 ten	*21 twenty-one*	*1,000,000 a million*

- Es gibt drei Möglichkeiten, die **Zahl 0** auszusprechen: 'nought' (v.a. in Großbritannien), 'zero' (v.a. in den USA) und 'oh' (in Zahlenreihen wie Telefonnummern, v.a. in Großbritannien).

- Vorsicht: Man schreibt 'f**ou**r' und 'f**ou**rteen', aber 'f**o**rty'!

- Die Zahlen **'hundred', 'thousand', 'million'** etc. stehen i.d.R. im **Singular,** z.B.

  How many people are unemployed in Germany? Over four million?

- In Großbritannien steht **'and' zwischen 'hundred' und dem Rest der Zahl,** z.B. 'five hundred and sixty-six'. US-Amerikaner sagen 'five hundred sixty-six'.

- **Zahlen über Tausend** werden i.d.R. mit **Komma** geschrieben. Einen **Punkt** benutzt man für **Dezimalstellen,** z.B.

  1,549 *('one thousand five hundred (and) forty-nine')*
  3.75 % *('three point seven five per cent')*

Ordnungszahlen:

1st	*the first*	*12th*	*the twelfth*	*23rd*	*the twenty-third*
2nd	*the second*	*13th*	*the thirteenth*	*30th*	*the thirtieth*
3rd	*the third*	*14th*	*the fourteenth*	*40th*	*the fortieth*
4th	*the fourth*	*15th*	*the fifteenth*	*50th*	*the fiftieth*
5th	*the fifth*	*16th*	*the sixteenth*	*60th*	*the sixtieth*
6th	*the sixth*	*17th*	*the seventeenth*	*70th*	*the seventieth*
7th	*the seventh*	*18th*	*the eighteenth*	*80th*	*the eightieth*
8th	*the eighth*	*19th*	*the nineteenth*	*90th*	*the ninetieth*
9th	*the ninth*	*20th*	*the twentieth*	*100th*	*the hundredth*
10th	*the tenth*	*21st*	*the twenty-first*	*200th*	*the two hundredth*
11th	*the eleventh*	*22nd*	*the twenty-second*	*1,000th*	*the thousandth*

- Charles **III** heißt 'Charles **the Third**'.

54 Exercises

I. Write out these numbers using the words you would use to say them. ●●

1. 105
2. 99.9
3. 1,378
4. 10,529
5. 560,000

II. Complete these sentences using a number. Write it out in full. ●●

1. There are … players in a football team but … in a rugby team.
2. How many … are there in a billion? Nine or twelve?
3. They say that life begins at … .
4. Do you think more money should be given to the … World?
5. The normal age of retirement for men is … .
6. Why do people treat foreigners as …-class citizens?
7. Applications (*Bewerbungen*) will be dealt with on a … come, … served basis.
8. Did you have a special party on your … birthday?
9. Do you know the expression: '…'s company, …'s a crowd'?
10. British people have fireworks on … November, Guy Fawkes' Night.

55 Datum und Uhrzeit (Time and date)

- Es gibt drei Möglichkeiten, nach dem **Datum** zu **fragen:**

What's today's date, please?
What date is it today, please?
What's the date today, please?

- Folgende **Antworten** sind möglich:

'December the ninth' (BE) *'ninth December'* (AE)
'the ninth of December' (BE) *'December ninth'* (AE)

- Bei **Jahresangaben** sagt man:

'Nineteen ninety-eight' (1998) *'Two thousand and one'* (2001)

- Unterschiede in der **Kurzschreibweise,** z.B.

Date	BE	AE
9 December 1998	9/12/98	12/9/98

- Bei der **Uhrzeit** wichtige Unterschiede, z.B.

Time	BE	AE
3.00	*'three (o'clock)'*	*'three (o'clock)'*
3.15	*'three fifteen'/'(a) quarter past three'*	*'(a) quarter after three'*
3.20	*'twenty past three'*	*'twenty after three'*
3.30	*'half (past) three'*	*'half past three'*
3.45	*'(a) quarter to four'*	*'(a) quarter of four'*

- **'o'clock'** steht nur bei **voller Stunde** und entfällt in der Umgangsprache ganz.

- Um bei der **'12-hour clock'** deutlich zu machen, ob Vormittag, Nachmittag oder Abend gemeint ist, fügt man **'in the morning', 'in the afternoon'** oder **'in the evening'** hinzu. Die Abkürzungen **'a.m.'** (lat. 'ante meridiem') und **'p.m.'** (lat. 'post meridiem') benutzt man nur im geschriebenen Englisch, z.B.

'We've got a meeting at nine-thirty in the afternoon,' she says.
The meeting begins at 9.30 a.m.

- Die **'24-hour clock'** verwendet man i.d.R. nur in **Fahrplänen.**

55 Exercises

I. Write out these dates in the way you would say them. (Why are these dates so important in American history?) ●●

1. 4 July 1776
2. 25 June 1876
3. 22 November 1963
4. 4 April 1968

II. Complete this well-known rhyme with four numbers. ●●

… days has September,
April, June and November,
All the rest have … ,
Except February alone,
Which has but … days clear,
And … in each Leap Year.

III. Write down the German for the following. (Use a dictionary if you wish.)

1. a fortnight
2. a leap year
3. Boxing Day
4. bank holiday
5. Whitsun

IV. Read this extract from a novel. ●●

In 1935 'the gang' were certainly all kids, between sixteen and twenty-one or -two. And in 1938 they still called themselves kids, though in the daytime, between the hours of eight and four or four-thirty, these children were ambitious young businessmen, rising civil servants, and the girls were their secretaries; and if someone demanded, 'Where's Bobby, why haven't we seen Bobby lately?', the girl who felt herself responsible for him would say with a faraway, devoted look in her eyes, 'He's got an exam,' and everyone nodded (*nickte*) understandingly, with a sympathetic sigh (*Seufzer*).

(From *Martha Quest* by Doris Lessing)

Lösungen (Key)

1 Exercises

I. **1.** a – A – an – **2.** an – a – **3.** a – **4.** a – an – **5.** an – **6.** an – **7.** An – a – **8.** an

II. **1.** an – a – **2.** an – a – **3.** a – a – **4.** a – **5.** a – **6.** an – **7.** a – an – **8.** a – a

III. **1.** a journalist – **2.** a nurse – **3.** a pilot – **4.** a teacher – **5.** a hairdresser – **6.** a musician/a violinist

IV. **1.** I go swimming three times a week. – **2.** Sugar costs £1.70 a kilo. – **3.** It's a pity (that) she can't come. – **4.** Can you give me a piece of advice?

2 Exercises

I. **1.** ∅ – **2.** ∅ – **3.** ∅ – **4.** ∅ – the – **5.** ∅ – the – **6.** ∅ – **7.** ∅ – ∅ – **8.** the – ∅

II. **1.** ∅ – **2.** ∅ – **3.** ∅ – **4.** the – **5.** the – **6.** ∅ – **7.** ∅ – **8.** the

III. **1.** ∅ – the – **2.** ∅ – **3.** ∅ – The – **4.** ∅ – ∅ – **5.** ∅ – the – **6.** ∅

IV. **1.** There is no alternative to peace. – **2.** Death is a necessary end. – **3.** Life can be so pleasant. – **4.** Modern society thinks differently.

3 Exercises

I. **1.** ladies – gentlemen – children – **2.** boxes – taxis – **3.** women – jobs – **4.** lorries – streets – **5.** people – offices – **6.** wishes – **7.** oranges – strawberries – **8.** parties

II. **1.** Are these your tomatoes? – **2.** They are young children. – **3.** Dublin('s) buses are green. – **4.** There are no leaves on those trees. – **5.** This disco is fantastic! – **6.** Does your tooth hurt? – **7.** A man can't have a baby. – **8.** You left your book on my shelf.

III. **1.** mothers-in-law – **2.** sheep – **3.** women drivers – **4.** lives – **5.** analyses

IV. Water was the most active thing in the valley, arriving in the long rains from Wales. It would drop all day from clouds and trees, from roofs and eaves and noses. It broke open roads, carved its way through gardens, and filled the ditches with sucking noises.

4 Exercises

I. **1.** some – **2.** some – **3.** is – it – **4.** isn't – hasn't

II. **1.** Is – **2.** Does – **3.** Is – **4.** Has

III. **1.** The information about Ireland (which) we received was very interesting. – **2.** He needs (some) new glasses/spectacles. – **3.** Many thanks for the advice you gave us. – **4.** Do you want another slice/piece of toast or another piece/ slice of cake?

IV. **1.** b. – **2.** a.

V. The noun 'police' is used with a plural verb form. (*Example*: Look! The police are coming.)

5 Exercises

I. **1.** Chris's – **2.** ladies' – **3.** men's – boys' – **4.** brothers' – names – **5.** St. James's – **6.** children's – **7.** doctor's – **8.** parents' (zu 1. u. 5.: 's wird i.d.R. selbst bei Eigennamen angefügt, die auf -s enden.)

II. **1.** Germany's exports – **2.** this evening's football matches – **3.** The world's population – **4.** England's largest city – **5.** last Saturday's *Times* – **6.** The company's success

III. **1.** The door of the room – **2.** The beginning of the play/The play's beginning – **3.** the hands of the clock – **4.** the end of the world – **5.** the third floor of the building – **6.** the top of every page

IV. **1.** d. – **2.** e. – **3.** a. – **4.** b. – **5.** c.

6 Exercises

I. **1.** you – **2.** it – **3.** them – **4.** it – **5.** me – **6.** me – **7.** him – **8.** he

II. **1.** right – **2.** lovely – **3.** use – **4.** necessary – **5.** important – **6.** difficult

III. **1.** is – **2.** has – **3.** is – **4.** is

IV. **1.** the government – **2.** the French/British – **3.** the manufacturers – **4.** people

7 Exercises

I. **1.** mine – **2.** yours – **3.** hers – **4.** His – **5.** Ours/Mine

II. **1.** myself – **2.** yourselves – **3.** yourself/yourselves – **4.** yourself – **5.** yourself

III. **1.** each other – **2.** themselves – **3.** yourself – **4.** one another – **5.** ourselves – each other

8 Exercises

I. **1.** d. – **2.** e. – **3.** b. – **4.** c. – **5.** a.

II. **1.** When did the train arrive? – **2.** Why didn't he come to the meeting? – **3.** Who phoned you last night? – **4.** Who did Jenny see yesterday afternoon? – **5.** Whose mistake was it?

III. **1.** Who is the present from? – **2.** What must we write about? – **3.** Where do you come from? – **4.** Who is this letter for? – **5.** Which chair can I sit on?

IV. **1.** these – **2.** that – **3.** those – **4.** This – **5.** those – **6.** that

9 Exercises

I. **1.** who – **2.** which – **3.** who – **4.** which – **5.** which – **6.** who –
In three sentences: 1. – 3. – 4.

II. **1.** where – **2.** whose – **3.** where – **4.** who – **5.** where – **6.** where

III. **1.** ∅ – **2.** ∅ – **3.** ∅ – **4.** who – **5.** who – **6.** that

10 Exercises

I. **1.** someone/somebody – **2.** anything – **3.** some – **4.** any – **5.** any – **6.** some – **7.** anything – **8.** anybody

II. **1.** much – **2.** many – **3.** a lot of – **4.** much/a lot of – **5.** much – **6.** a lot of – much – **7.** A lot of/Many – **8.** many

III. **1.** a few – **2.** a little – **3.** a few – **4.** a little

IV. **1.** every – **2.** each – **3.** Many – **4.** several

11 Exercises

I. **1.** thinner – **2.** more important – **3.** more serious – **4.** happier – **5.** most expensive – **6.** more quiet/quieter – **7.** busier – **8.** easier – better

II. **1.** best – **2.** most intelligent – **3.** most embarrassing – **4.** happiest – **5.** most demanding

III. **1.** f. – **2.** e. – **3.** c. – **4.** b. – **5.** d.

IV. **1.** The queue is getting longer and longer. – **2.** Eating out is getting more and more expensive. – **3.** Life is getting more and more complicated. – **4.** The world is getting smaller and smaller.

12 Exercises

I. **1.** constantly – **2.** easily – **3.** brilliantly – **4.** hard – **5.** positively – **6.** regularly – **7.** extremely well – **8.** badly – immediately

II. **1.** quietly – lightly – **2.** loudly – enthusiastically – **3.** angry – exactly – **4.** frequently – locally – **5.** bitterly – **6.** well – fluently – **7.** excellent – **8.** slow – quickly

III. loudly – hardly – differently – properly – hard – seriously – immediately – really – happy – nice

13 Exercises

I. **1.** at – **2.** on – at – **3.** on – **4.** in – **5.** on – **6.** in

II. **1.** with – **2.** on – **3.** in – **4.** on – **5.** on – **6.** to – **7.** in – **8.** at

III. **1.** on – **2.** for – **3.** by – **4.** on – **5.** at – **6.** of

IV. **1.** until – **2.** Although – **3.** in order to – **4.** because – **5.** since – **6.** Before – **7.** whether – **8.** after

14 Exercises

I. **1.** full verb – **2.** primary auxiliary – **3.** full verb – **4.** primary auxiliary – **5.** primary auxiliary – **6.** full verb – **7.** full verb – **8.** primary auxiliary

II. 4.

III. 1. – 4.

IV. 3.

15 Exercises

I. **1.** fact – **2.** opinion

II. **1.** feeling – **2.** fact

III. **1.** attitude – **2.** fact

IV. **1.** fact – **2.** judgement

V. **1.** request – **2.** permission – **3.** possibility – **4.** offer – **5.** refusal – **6.** suggestion – **7.** invitation – **8.** deduction

16 Exercises

I. **1.** Can you use a computer? – **2.** Could you lend me some money? – **3.** Can you speak French? – **4.** Can I help you with your homework? – **5.** Can you play a musical instrument? – **6.** Can I offer you a drink? – **7.** Could I use the dictionary? – **8.** Can you give me some advice?

II. 1. – 2. – 4. – 6.

III. **1.** He might be at home. – **2.** It might rain later. – **3.** We might go to England in the summer. – **4.** She might have time. – **5.** They might give us a lift to the airport. – **6.** We might move house next year.

IV. **1.** must – **2.** mustn't – **3.** mustn't – **4.** must – **5.** must – **6.** mustn't

17 Exercises

I. **1.** I think you should go to the dentist. – **2.** … learn some English. – **3.** … look for a new job. – **4.** … stop smoking.

II. **1.** c. – **2.** d. – **3.** b. – **4.** a.

III. **1.** d. – **2.** f. – **3.** h. – **4.** b. – **5.** c. – **6.** e.

18 Exercises

I. **1.** a. – **2.** b. – **3.** a. – **4.** b. – **5.** b. – **6.** a. – **7.** a. – **8.** b.

II. **1.** mustn't – **2.** didn't have to – **3.** don't have to – **4.** don't have to – **5.** don't have to – **6.** mustn't

III. 2. (In sentences 1 and 3 the speaker uses the modal auxiliaries 'must' and 'will'. These show that the speaker is personally 'involved' in the obligation. In sentence 2 the obligation is from 'outside'.)

19 Exercises

I. Past: 2. – 3. – 5. – 6. – Future: 1. – 4.

II. **1.** can't have taken – **2.** may not have understood – **3.** might not have told – **4.** must have left – **5.** should have arrived – **6.** should not have said – **7.** might not have gone out – **8.** must have had

20 Exercises

I. **1.** was able to play – **2.** were able to lend – **3.** have never been able to understand – **4.** were not able to see – **5.** has not been able to go

II. **1.** were not allowed to watch – **2.** Are English children allowed to wear – **3.** didn't have to pay – **4.** Are all English shops allowed to open – **5.** is not allowed to get

III. **1.** Have you ever had to go – **2.** had to stay – **3.** Did you have to say – **4.** have to go – **5.** do you have to get up

IV. **1.** don't have to wait – **2.** mustn't forget – **3.** must come and see – **4.** don't have to travel

21 Exercises

I. **1.** b. – **2.** c. – **3.** a. – **4.** b. – **5.** a.

II. **1.** used to write – **2.** used to play – **3.** used to smoke – **4.** used to go – **5.** used to have

III. **1.** d. I'd rather have dinner at home. – **2.** g. I'd rather come at four. – **3.** e. I'd rather have it now. – **4.** c. I'd rather go immediately. – **5.** b. I'd rather walk the whole way.

22 Exercises

I. **1.** How many children has Daniel got? – **2.** Where have Patricia and Malcolm got a house? – **3.** When has Francis got a free evening? – **4.** What didn't they have in the corner shop? – **5.** Why did Jackie have a car in London?

II. **1.** Excuse me? Have you got the time? – **2.** Excuse me? Have you got a light? – **3.** Excuse me? Have you got some change for £5? – **4.** Excuse me? Have you got a pen/something to write with? – **5.** Excuse me? Have you got a stamp (with you)?

III. **1.** Do you have a minute? – **2.** She has a good job. – **3.** Do they have a pet? – **4.** We don't have many good friends. – **5.** He is having lunch.

IV. **1.** Did you have a swim this morning? – **2.** They haven't got their own car! – **3.** Have you got many public holidays in your country? – **4.** They have got their passports with them. – **5.** He hasn't got a beard, just a moustache.

23 Exercises

I. **1.** Must we leave now? – **2.** Is she working in the States? – **3.** Did he take a taxi? – **4.** Can they speak English fluently? – **5.** Have we been living here for a long time? – **6.** Is health more important than wealth? – **7.** Did they have to go by car? – **8.** Does it look like it's going to be a nice day?

II. **1.** Yes, I do. – **2.** No, she wasn't. – **3.** Yes, they do. – **4.** No, he won't. – **5.** No, they haven't. – **6.** Yes, we are. – **7.** Yes, they were. – **8.** No, they didn't.

III. **1.** …, aren't you? – **2.** …, hasn't he? – **3.** …, does she? – **4.** …, hadn't you? – **5.** …, do I? – **6.** …, weren't you? – **7.** …, will you? – **8.** …, aren't we?

24 Exercises

I.

Time	Verb form
1. present	past continuous
2. present	present perfect continuous
3. future	past simple
4. past	past simple
5. present	past perfect simple

II. Four verbs (in sentences 1. – 2. – 5. – 6.)

III. They are all perfect forms: **1.** present perfect simple – **2.** present perfect simple – **3.** future perfect simple – **4.** past perfect simple – **5.** present perfect continuous – **6.** past perfect simple – **7.** present perfect simple – **8.** future perfect simple

25 Exercises

I. **1.** knows – likes – **2.** says – are – is – **3.** like – don't like – **4.** goes – is – **5.** haven't got – can't – **6.** work – don't earn – **7.** doesn't drink – prefers – **8.** isn't – think – is

II. **1.** What does the German word ‚Bauchredner' mean in English? ('ventriloquist') – **2.** When does he get home every evening except Friday? – **3.** Where does she live now? – **4.** How does he get to school? – **5.** Why does he speak so loudly all the time? – **6.** Whose pen is this? – **7.** Who do they see every weekend throughout the whole year? – **8.** What colour are her eyes?/ What colour eyes has she got?

III. **1.** We are often in England. – **2.** We usually fly there. – **3.** We sometimes go to London. – **4.** We normally stay there for a week. – **5.** We would never stay in big hotels. – **6.** They are usually far too expensive.

IV. Number 3 is the odd one out: 'say' is pronounced /seɪ/ but 'says' is pronounced /sez/.

26 Exercises

I. **1.** am trying – **2.** is making – **3.** are looking – **4.** is not working – **5.** is snowing

II. 4.

III. Clare: are you doing – Rick: am studying – Clare: are you studying – Clare: Are you enjoying – Rick: am learning – Clare: am applying – Clare: don't think – Clare: don't want

27 Exercises

I. **1.** bit – **2.** had – **3.** saw – **4.** drank – **5.** slept

II. **1.** Where did you go last night? – **2.** How did you get there? – **3.** What did you see? – **4.** Did you enjoy it? – **5.** Why were you (so) late?

III. saw – had – was – thought – spoke – liked – heard – began – fell – caught – ate – laughed – ran

28 Exercises

I. **1.** was having – **2.** were playing – **3.** was driving – **4.** was lying – **5.** were arguing – **6.** was sitting – (was) writing – **7.** were watching – **8.** was mowing

II. **1.** Where were you living five years ago? – **2.** Were you living alone? – **3.** Were you working at that time? – **4.** Were you doing the job you wanted? – **5.** Were you earning enough money? – **6.** Were you enjoying life as much as now?

III. **1.** was travelling – met – **2.** Were you sitting – phoned – **3.** were you laughing – came – **4.** were waiting – began – **5.** got – were living – **6.** stole – was shopping – **7.** was leaving – rang – **8.** was falling – came – woke

IV. went – got – carried – wandered – was – was blowing

29 Exercises

I. **1.** I've just had one. – **2.** I've known him for years. – **3.** I've pulled a muscle. – **4.** I've been here for six months. – **5.** I've just passed my exams. – **6.** I've sold it to a friend. – **7.** I've never been there before. – **8.** I've not read it yet.

II. **1.** since – **2.** for – **3.** for – **4.** since – **5.** since – **6.** for – **7.** since – **8.** since

III. **1.** We've just arrived. – **2.** I haven't seen the film yet. – **3.** Have you ever been to Cornwall? – **4.** I've heard that joke before./I've already heard that joke. – **5.** We've never gone through the Channel Tunnel.

IV. **1.** Wie lange bist du/sind Sie noch hier? – **2.** Wie lange bist du/sind Sie schon hier?

30 Exercises

I. **1.** Who has/Who's been eating my porridge? – **2.** Who's been sitting on my chair? – **3.** Who's been sleeping in my bed?

II. **1.** Somebody has/Somebody's eaten all my porridge! – **2.** Somebody's broken my chair! – **3.** Somebody's been sleeping in my bed and she is still there!

III. **1.** a. – **2.** b. – **3.** b. – **4.** a. – **5.** b. – **6.** a. – **7.** a. – **8.** b. – **9.** a. – **10.** b.

31 Exercises

I. **1.** b. it had closed at midnight. – **2.** a. I had never met her before. – **3.** e. they had already gone home. – **4.** c. the bus had been late. – **5.** d. I had never flown before.

II. **1.** after – **2.** when – **3.** because – **4.** before – **5.** as

III. was – was going – was married – didn't care – was – had developed – knew – had received

32 Exercises

I. **1.** A lot of people had been smoking. – **2.** She had been dreaming. – **3.** He had been cycling in the rain. – **4.** They had been running. – **5.** She had been reading a book about them.

II. **1.** a. – **2.** b. – **3.** a. – **4.** b. – **5.** b. – **6.** a. – **7.** b. – **8.** a.

III. **1.** After the plane had been flying for an hour, there was an engine failure. – **2.** After he had been driving for eight hours, he fell asleep at the wheel and crashed. – **3.** After she had been cycling for forty minutes, she got cramp in her leg and had to stop. – **4.** After they had been trying to hitchhike for two minutes, somebody picked them up. – **5.** After they had been playing loud music for two hours, the neighbour complained about the noise. – **6.** After the children had been reading together for ten minutes, an argument broke out.

33 Exercises

I. **1.** a. – **2.** b. – **3.** a. – **4.** a.

II. **1.** contains – **2.** look – **3.** hates – doesn't mind – **4.** Does anyone want – **5.** does she come – **6.** Do you really love – **7.** don't understand – mean – **8.** want – don't want

III. **1.** are you thinking – **2.** do you think – **3.** Does your brother have/Has your brother got – **4.** Is your brother having – **5.** look – **6.** are looking – **7.** Is he seeing – **8.** Does he see/Can he see

34 Exercises

I. 3. No, she's going to have a baby!
II. 4. Yes, we're dancing./1. Yes, we will be dancing.
III. 2. I'll have a gin and tonic, please.
IV. 2. I'm going to get fit.

35 Exercises

I. **1.** non-modal – **2.** modal – **3.** non-modal – **4.** non-modal
II. **1.** I'll be ringing – **2.** Will she be waiting – **3.** We'll be arriving – **4.** Will you be spending
III. **1.** will have closed – **2.** will have spent – **3.** will have finished – **4.** will have learnt
IV. **1.** will have been doing – **2.** will have been driving – **3.** will have been living – **4.** will have been working

36 Exercises

I. **1.** I'll – **2.** I'll – **3.** I'm going (to go) to – **4.** I'll – **5.** I'll – **6.** are you going to get
II. Spontaneous: 1. – 2. – 4. – 6. – Neutral: 3. – 5.
III. **1**a. – **2**b. – **3**b. – **4**b. – **5**b.

37 Exercises

I. Present time: 1. – 3. – 8. – Future time: 2. – 4. – 5. – 6. – 7.
II. **1.** Which day is your birthday on this year? – **2.** When do supermarkets in Britain close in the evening? – **3.** Which hotel is he staying at? – **4.** How often are there flights to Philadelphia in summer? – **5.** When do you think our train leaves? – **6.** Who are you having a holiday with? – **7.** Who is organizing a party at Christmas? – **8.** Why is she going back to live with her parents?
III. am looking after – is picking – are driving – are stopping – are carrying on – begins – lasts – are – starts

38 Exercises

I. **1.** Our pet cat was run over by a car last night. – **2.** A 23-year-old soldier was shot in Londonderry. – **3.** My central heating is being repaired today. – **4.** This carpet was made in India. – **5.** Photographs may not be taken in this theatre. – **6.** Have you been invited to our party? – **7.** English is spoken almost everywhere. – **8.** My car has been stolen!
II. **1.** She was thanked. – **2.** We weren't promised anything. – **3.** We were told to come at nine o'clock. – **4.** They were given a present. – **5.** She was shown the

town. – **6.** We were asked to write a short report. – **7.** We were taken to the airport. – **8.** They were taught a new card game.

III. There is one passive form ('had been found'). There are not any more passive forms because the passage describes what the main character does, not what happens to her.

39 Exercises

I. 'have sth done': 1. – 3. – 5. – Past perfect simple: 2. – 4. – 6.

II. **1.** has had it cleaned – **2.** has had it cut – **3.** has had it repaired – **4.** is having them developed – **5.** is having a photograph taken – **6.** has it delivered – **7.** has had it painted – **8.** to have them sent

III. **1.** We had the television bought for us. – **2.** He has all the rugby matches recorded for him. – **3.** Anita is having her printer repaired. – **4.** Mrs Fleming has had her hedges cut. – **5.** Stephen and Clare had their wedding photos taken by a professional photographer. – **6.** Alison had had her eyes tested before she bought her new glasses. – **7.** Penny always has her hair cut at home. – **8.** Charley has had the tickets for the jazz concert sent to his home address.

40 Exercises

I. **1.** f. hereinschauen – **2.** e. aufbleiben – **3.** h. hervorragend sein – **4.** a. über Kreuz sein mit – **5.** c. einschlafen – **6.** b. herumkommen – **7.** d. besser werden – **8.** g. sich in Schale werfen

II. **1.** She broke off the relationship. – **2.** He has given up smoking. – **3.** We need to step up production. – **4.** I think you made (up) that story (up)! – **5.** The explosion wiped (out) the village (out). – **6.** Can you dish out these leaflets to the houses in your street? – **7.** Do you know who set up this scheme by the way? – **8.** We were held up in London because of the fog.

III. **1.** d. – **2.** j. – **3.** h. – **4.** f. – **5.** c. – **6.** b. – **7.** e. – **8.** a.

41 Exercises

I. **1.** of getting – **2.** to get – **3.** to get – **4.** to get – **5.** getting

II. **1.** to find – **2.** in finding – **3.** to find – **4.** to find – **5.** of finding

III. **1.** to accept – **2.** accepting – **3.** to accept – **4.** to accept – **5.** to accept

42 Exercises

I. **1.** want – I'll get – **2.** goes – will we be – **3.** I'll sit – don't mind – **4.** won't go running – keeps – **5.** does milk keep – isn't – **6.** don't have – won't be able

II. **1.** made – **2.** had – **3.** went – **4.** knew/spoke – **5.** were

III. **1.** had told – would certainly have waited – **2.** would have come round and seen – had had – **3.** would have lent – had saved – **4.** had been – would not have had – **5.** had not been – would probably have got to – **6.** would have helped – had asked

IV. 'had': 1. – 3. – 'would': 2. – 4.

43 Exercises

I. **1.** I wish it would stop raining. – **2.** I wish someone would answer the telephone. – **3.** I wish they wouldn't play their music so loudly. – **4.** I wish he wouldn't drive so dangerously. – **5.** I wish the taxi would come. – **6.** I wish she/he would call.

II. **1.** I wish I had more friends. – **2.** I wish I drove my own car. – **3.** I wish I earned more money. – **4.** I wish I lived in the city. – **5.** I wish I looked fit. – **6.** I wish I knew enough English words.

III. **1.** I wish I had known him better. – **2.** I wish we had had a warmer summer. – **3.** I wish I had got on better with my brothers. – **4.** I wish I had taken a holiday last year. – **5.** I wish we had been at home when they called. – **6.** I wish they had invited us to the wedding.

44 Exercises

I. **1.** He said (that) his sister had a new boyfriend. – **2.** … he had bought a new mountain bike. – **3.** … he didn't know where Joe was living. – **4.** … he was going to Rachel's wedding on (the following) Saturday. – **5.** … he had been trying to get fit recently. – **6.** … we could go out together on (the following) Friday night. – **7.** … his father had retired. – **8.** … his job was getting so boring.

II. **1.** told – **2.** said – **3.** told – **4.** talked – **5.** said – **6.** talked – **7.** told – **8.** told

III. **1.** Richard said (that) he was leaving Germany after Christmas. – **2.** Donna told Ray (that) he was crazy and (that) it wouldn't work. – **3.** Catherine was told (that) Anna had paid for the meal. – **4.** The receptionist explained that dinner was served between seven and ten. – **5.** Jason explained that it had taken him an hour longer than usual to get there.

45 Exercises

I. **1.** b. – c. – d. – **2.** a. – b. – **3.** a. – b.

II. **1.** a. Sally suggested that Clive should take the job. – **1.** b. Sally advised Clive to take the job. – **2.** a. The teacher recommended that Kevin should study. – **2.** b. The teacher wanted Kevin to study. – **3.** a. The boss asked

David to give him the documents. – **3.** b. The boss ordered David to give him the documents. – **4.** a. Her father expected Sue to visit him. – **4.** b. Her father insisted on Sue visiting him.

III. **1.** He asked Jane if she had been there the day before/the previous day. – **2.** She asked Paul if he was coming the following day/the day after. – **3.** She said (that) she had been there two hours before. – **4.** He said (that) he loved her.

46 Exercises

I. Defining: 2. – 3. – 5. – Non-defining: 1. – 4. – 6.

II. **1.** … (which/that) Craig is wearing. – **2.** … where Kim's parents stayed wasn't too expensive. – **3.** … (which/that) we were served for breakfast was sour. – **4.** … is the only person who/that understands me. – **5.** … (which/that) Trevor went to was very loud and overcrowded. – **6.** … (which/that) Lucy has applied for is in Sweden. – **7.** … (which/that) we wanted tickets for was sold out. – **8.** … who/that answered the phone told me you were at work.

47 Exercises

I. **1.** Travelling (s) – **2.** cheating (s) – **3.** Having (s) – **4.** skiing (o) – ice-skating (o) – **5.** answering (o) – **6.** living (o) – **7.** walking (o) – **8.** talking (o) – looking (o)

II. **1.** for being – **2.** of reading – on watching – **3.** for ruining – **4.** of emigrating – **5.** of being – **6.** of hurting – **7.** at playing – at performing – **8.** on doing

48 Exercises

I. **1.** would like to have – **2.** didn't dare to laugh – **3.** decision to go – **4.** mustn't leave – **5.** am not able to get – **6.** too old to go – **7.** decided to wait – **8.** dangerous to play

II. **1.** Can you please tell me where to park? – **2.** We really don't know which book to take. – **3.** Do you know how to find out more about British universities? – **4.** It's warm enough to eat outside. – **5.** The best thing for me would be to find a job. – **6.** The tea is too strong for me to drink.

III. **1.** me to help – **2.** her to think – **3.** him not to go – **4.** them to hurry up – **5.** you to have – **6.** him to finish – **7.** her to drive – **8.** us to borrow

49 Exercises

I. **1.** keen on doing/keen to do – **2.** afraid of making/afraid to make – **3.** way of finding/way to find – **4.** for being – **5.** chance of leaving/chance to leave

II. Past: 1. – 2. – 4. – 5. – 6. – Present: 3.
III. **1.** a. – **2.** b. – **3.** b. – **4.** a. – **5.** b. – **6.** a.
IV. 2. (It is unlikely that you will see something burn as a whole action, i.e. from beginning to end.)

50 Exercises

I. **1.** I got home feeling tired. – **2.** The man sat on the park bench talking to himself. – **3.** He cut himself peeling onions. – **4.** 'Is this seat free?' he asked, pointing to a chair next to her. – **5.** They were in London visiting their daughter. – **6.** I often spend the evening at home, listening to music or reading. – **7.** She came into the room, looking around and smiling. – **8.** He ran into the house, shouting and waving his arms.
II. **1.** Who is the old woman living opposite you? – **2.** I'd like to get a job offering better career opportunities. – **3.** Do you know about the problems facing the environment? – **4.** Identify the sentences containing a participle construction. – **5.** Did you see that car driving over the red lights? – **6.** Although being ill, she went to work.
III. **1.** The train which/that is arriving at platform 5 is the 10.15 from Bristol Parkway. – **2.** People who/that are travelling to work on the M25 … – **3.** They were given a room which/that overlooks/overlooked Hyde Park. – **4.** Models who/that reach the top of their profession … – **5.** Did you see that man outside the bank who/that was holding a big suitcase?
IV. Time: 4. – Reason: 1. – 2. – 3.
V. **1.** Weil sie für ihr Vorstellungsgespräch schon verspätet war, hatte Kate keine Zeit mehr zum Frühstücken. – **2.** Es ist ärgerlich, zu spät zu einem Vorstellungsgespräch zu kommen.

51 Exercises

I. **1.** Books borrowed from … – **2.** Toni Morrison's first book, written in … – **3.** Some animals hunted for … – **4.** The advice given to … – **5.** The jobs offered to …
II. **1.** Most of the clothes which/that are sold … – **2.** All letters which/that are posted … – **3.** The people who/that were injured … – **4.** The houses which/that were built … – **5.** The window which/that was broken …
III. **1.** f. – **2.** e. – **3.** d. – **4.** a. – **5.** c. – **6.** b.

52 Exercises

I. **1.** after – **2.** while – **3.** When – **4.** as soon as
II. **1.** e. – **2.** b. – **3.** a. – **4.** d.

III. **1.** because – **2.** although – **3.** although – **4.** because
IV. **1.** gets – **2.** am – **3.** see – **4.** go

53 Exercises

I. **1.** He just went home. – **2.** Did she speak to you yet? – **3.** Do you have a problem? – **4.** Shall we meet at twenty after two? – **5.** What will the weather be like on the weekend?
II. **1.** liter – **2.** favor – **3.** check – **4.** defense – **5.** whiskey – **6.** to analyze
III. **1.** gas – **2.** fall – **3.** fries – **4.** elevator – **5.** candy – **6.** sidewalk – **7.** vacation – **8.** garbage – **9.** downtown – **10.** store

54 Exercises

I. **1.** 'one hundred and five' – **2.** 'ninty-nine point nine' – **3.** 'one thousand three hundred and seventy-eight' – **4.** 'ten thousand five hundred and twenty-nine' – **5.** 'five hundred and sixty thousand'
II. **1.** eleven – fifteen – **2.** noughts/zeros – **3.** forty – **4.** Third – **5.** sixty-five – **6.** second – **7.** first – first – **8.** eighteenth – **9.** two – three – **10.** the fifth of

55 Exercises

I. **1.** 'The fourth of July (BE)/July fourth (AE) seventeen seventy-six.' (Declaration of Independence in Philadelphia) – **2.** 'The twenty-fifth of June/June twenty-fifth eighteen seventy-six.' (Battle of the Little Bighorn, where Sioux Indians killed General Custer) – **3.** 'The twenty-second of November/November twenty-second nineteen sixty-three.' (J. F. Kennedy was assassinated in Dallas) – **4.** 'The fourth of April/April fourth nineteen sixty-eight.' (Assassination of Martin Luther King in Memphis)
II. Thirty – thirty-one – twenty-eight – twenty-nine
III. **1.** zwei Wochen (14 Tage) – **2.** ein Schaltjahr – **3.** 26. Dezember – **4.** ein öffentlicher Feiertag – **5.** Pfingsten

Unregelmäßige Verben (Irregular verbs)

(Die Formen in Klammern werden gewöhnlich im amerikanischen Englisch verwendet.)

abide, abided (abode), abided ausstehen, aushalten
arise, arose, arisen aufsteigen, sich erheben
awake, awoke, awoken (auf)wecken
be, was, been sein
bear, bore, borne (er)tragen
beat, beat, beaten (beat) schlagen
become, became, become werden
begin, began, begun anfangen, beginnen
bend, bent, bent biegen, krümmen
bet, bet (betted), bet (betted) wetten
bind, bound, bound binden
bite, bit, bitten beißen
bleed, bled, bled bluten
blow, blew, blown blasen, wehen
break, broke, broken (zer)brechen
breed, bred, bred hervorbringen, gebären
bring, brought, brought bringen
broadcast, broadcast, broadcast senden, übertragen
build, built, built bauen
burn, burnt, burnt (ver)brennen
burst, burst, burst bersten, (zer)platzen
buy, bought, bought kaufen
catch, caught, caught fangen, erwischen
choose, chose, chosen (aus)wählen
cling, clung, clung kleben, haften
come, came, come kommen
cost, cost, cost kosten
creep, crept, crept kriechen, schleichen
cut, cut, cut schneiden
deal, dealt, dealt handeln
dig, dug, dug graben; forschen
dive, dived (dove), dived tauchen
do, did, done tun, machen
draw, drew, drawn zeichnen
dream, dreamed (dreamt), dreamed (dreamt) träumen
drink, drank, drunk trinken
drive, drove, driven fahren
dwell, dwelt (dwelled), dwelt (dwelled) wohnen; sich aufhalten
eat, ate, eaten essen
fall, fell, fallen fallen
feed, fed, fed füttern
feel, felt, felt fühlen
fight, fought, fought kämpfen
find, found, found finden
flee, fled, fled fliehen
fly, flew, flown fliegen
forbid, forbade (forbad), forbidden verbieten
forecast, forecast, forecast voraussagen
foretell, foretold, foretold vorhersagen
forget, forgot, forgotten vergessen
forgive, forgave, forgiven vergeben, verzeihen
freeze, froze, frozen (ge)frieren
get, got, got (gotten) bekommen; werden
give, gave, given geben
go, went, gone gehen
grind, ground, ground schleifen, schärfen
grow, grew, grown wachsen

hang, hung (hanged), hung (hanged) (auf)hängen
have, had, had haben, besitzen
hear, heard, heard hören
hide, hid, hidden (hid) verbergen, verstecken
hit, hit, hit schlagen
hold, held, held halten
hurt, hurt, hurt verletzen
keep, kept, kept behalten, aufbewahren
knit, knitted (knit), knitted (knit) stricken
know, knew, known wissen, kennen
lay, laid, laid legen
lead, led, led führen, leiten
lean, leaned (leant), leaned (leant) (sich) lehnen
learn, learned (learnt), learned (learnt) lernen; erfahren
leave, left, left verlassen; überlassen
lend, lent, lent (ver)leihen
let, let, let lassen
lie, lay, lain liegen
light, lit (lighted), lit (lighted) anmachen, anzünden
lose, lost, lost verlieren
make, made, made machen, (veran)lassen
mean, meant, meant meinen, bedeuten
meet, met, met treffen, begegnen
mistake, mistook, mistaken verwechseln
misunderstand, misunderstood, misunderstood missverstehen
mow, mowed, mown (mowed) (ab)mähen, schneiden
outdo, outdid, outdone übertreffen
overcome, overcame, overcome überwinden, bezwingen
oversee, oversaw, overseen beaufsichtigen, überwachen
overtake, overtook, overtaken einholen; überholen
pay, paid, paid (be)zahlen
prove, proved, proved (proven) (sich) herausstellen, erweisen
put, put, put setzen, legen, stellen
read, read /red/, **read** /red/ lesen
rebuild, rebuilt, rebuilt wieder aufbauen
remake, remade, remade wieder machen, neu machen
rend, rent, rent (zer)reißen
rewrite, rewrote, rewritten neu schreiben; umschreiben
rid, rid (ridded), rid (ridded) befreien, frei machen
ride, rode, ridden fahren; reiten
ring, rang, rung läuten
rise, rose, risen steigen, sich erheben
run, ran, run rennen, laufen
saw, sawed, sawn (sawed) sägen
say, said, said sagen
see, saw, seen sehen
seek, sought, sought suchen
sell, sold, sold verkaufen
send, sent, sent senden, schicken
set, set, set (fest)setzen
sew, sewed, sewn (sewed) nähen
shake, shook, shaken schütteln, zittern
shear, sheared, shorn (sheared) scheren
shed, shed, shed (*Tränen*) vergießen
shine, shone (shined), shone (shined) scheinen, glänzen
shoot, shot, shot (er)schießen
show, showed, shown (showed) zeigen

shrink, shrank (shrunk), shrunk schrumpfen
shut, shut, shut (zu)schließen
sing, sang, sung singen
sink, sank (sunk), sunk sinken
sit, sat, sat sitzen
slay, slew, slain erschlagen, morden
sleep, slept, slept schlafen
smell, smelt (smelled), smelt (smelled) riechen
sow, sowed, sown (sowed) säen
speak, spoke, spoken sprechen
spell, spelt (spelled), spelt (spelled) buchstabieren; schreiben
spend, spent, spent verbringen, ausgeben
spill, spilt (spilled), spilt (spilled) aus-, verschütten
spin, spun (span), spun spinnen
spit, spat (spit), spat (spit) spucken
split, split, split spalten
spoil, spoiled (spoilt), spoiled (spoilt) verderben
spread, spread, spread (sich) ausbreiten
spring, sprang (sprung), sprung springen
stand, stood, stood stehen
steal, stole, stolen stehlen
stick, stuck, stuck kleben; stechen
stink, stank (stunk), stunk stinken
stride, strode, stridden schreiten
strike, struck, struck schlagen, stoßen
swear, swore, sworn schwören
sweep, swept, swept kehren, fegen
swell, swelled, swollen (swelled) (an)schwellen
swim, swam, swum schwimmen
swing, swang, swung schwingen
take, took, taken nehmen
teach, taught, taught lehren, unterrichten
tear, tore, torn (zer)reißen
tell, told, told erzählen, sagen
think, thought, thought denken
thrive, thrived (throve), thrived gedeihen; blühen; Erfolg haben
throw, threw, thrown werfen
unbend, unbent, unbent strecken
understand, understood, understood verstehen, begreifen
unwind, unwound, unwound (sich) abwickeln
uphold, upheld, upheld hochhalten, aufrecht halten
wake, woke (waked), woken (waked) (auf)wecken, aufwachen
waylay, waylaid, waylaid auflauern
wear, wore, worn (*Kleider*) tragen
weave, wove, woven weben, wirken
wed, wedded (wed), wedded (wed) ehelichen, (sich) vermählen
weep, wept, wept weinen
wet, wetted (wet), wetted (wet) benetzen, anfeuchten
win, won, won gewinnen
wind, wound, wound sich winden, sich schlängeln
withdraw, withdrew, withdrawn (sich) zurückziehen; entfernen
withhold, withheld, withheld zurück-, abhalten
withstand, withstood, withstood widerstehen; sich widersetzen
wring, wrung, wrung auswringen, auswinden
write, wrote, written schreiben

Grammatische Begriffe (Grammatical terms)

active verb form	aktive Form des Verbs	*I <u>call</u> you.*
adjective	Adjektiv (Eigenschaftswort)	*dark, yellow, tall*
adverb	Adverb (Umstandswort)	*very, always, slowly*
adverb of degree	Adverb des Grades	*very, extremely*
adverb of frequency	Adverb der Häufigkeit	*always, never, often*
adverb of manner	Adverb der Art und Weise	*slowly, carefully, well*
adverb of place	Adverb des Ortes	*at home, in bed, outside*
adverb of time	Adverb der Zeit	*now, soon, yesterday*
article	Artikel (Geschlechtswort)	*a, an, the*
aspect	Aspekt	(s. unit 24)
auxiliary	Hilfsverb	*do, can, must*
backshift of tenses	Zeitverschiebung	*'I <u>am</u> tired.' → He said he <u>was</u> tired.*
by-phrase	*by*-Fügung	*He was caught <u>by the police</u>.*
cardinal number	Grundzahl	*one, two, three*
comparative	Komparativ	*faster than, more expensive than*
complex sentence	Satzgefüge	*We can't come because we're busy.*
conditional sentence (if-sentence)	Bedingungssatz (*if*-Satz)	*<u>If you needed us,</u> we would come.*
conjunction	Konjunktion (Bindewort)	*and, or, but*
consonant	Konsonant (Mitlaut)	*b, d, f*
contact clause	Relativsatz ohne Relativpronomen	*I read the book <u>you gave me</u>.*
continuous form	Verlaufsform	*we are living, they were hoping*
coordinating conjunction	nebengeordnete Konjunktion	*and, but*
countable noun	zählbares Substantiv	*chair(s), apple(s), reason(s)*
defining relative clause	bestimmender Relativsatz	*The city <u>I like most</u> is Madrid.*
definite article	bestimmter Artikel	*the*
demonstrative pronoun	Demonstrativpronomen	*this, that, these, those*

direct object	direktes Objekt (wen oder was?)	*We drink coffee.*
direct speech	direkte Rede	*'Hello,' he said.*
dynamic verb	dynamisches Verb	*to sing, to drive, to jump*
future	Zukunft (Futur I)	*I will work. I will be working.*
future forms	Zeitformen der Zukunft	*will, going to*
future perfect	vollendete Zukunft (Futur II)	*I will have worked. I will have been working.*
gerund	Gerund (*-ing*-Form)	*She enjoys working.*
imperative	Imperativ (Befehlsform)	*Sit down! Don't move!*
indefinite article	unbestimmter Artikel	*a, an*
indirect object	indirektes Objekt (wem?)	*He gave his mother a present.*
indirect speech	indirekte Rede	*He said he was cold.*
infinitive	Infinitiv (Grundform des Verbs)	*to walk, to smoke, to write*
intonation	Satzmelodie	*What are you doing?*
inversion	Inversion (Umstellung)	*Can you drive? Are you there?*
irregular verb	unregelmäßiges Verb	*see - saw - seen*
modal auxiliary	modales Hilfsverb	*can, shall, would*
multi-word verb	zusammengesetztes Verb	*look at, get on with*
negation	Verneinung	*We don't eat meat.*
non-defining relative clause	nicht bestimmender Relativsatz	*Mrs Tyler, who lives next door, is nice.*
noun	Substantiv (Hauptwort)	*page, telephone, dog*
object	Objekt	*I can't hear you.*
of-phrase	*of*-Fügung	*the name of the paper*
ordinal number	Ordnungszahl	*first, second, third*
passive verb form	passive Form des Verbs	*I was called.*
past	Vergangenheit (Imperfekt)	*she lived, she was living*
past participle	Partizip Perfekt	*given, tried, understood*
past perfect	Vorvergangenheit (Plusquamperfekt)	*we had driven, we had been driving*
personal passive	persönliches Passiv	*He was offered the position.*

Grammatische Begriffe (Grammatical terms)

personal pronoun	Personalpronomen	*I, you, he, me, you, him*
phrasal verb	zusammengesetztes Verb	*look at, get on with*
plural	Mehrzahl	*faces, people, children*
possessive pronoun	Possessivpronomen	*my, your, her*
preposition	Präposition (Verhältniswort)	*to, in, on*
preposition of direction	Präposition der Richtung	*to church, into the shop*
preposition of place	Präposition des Ortes	*in the cinema, at the bank*
preposition of time	Präposition der Zeit	*on Sunday, in summer, at three o'clock*
present	Gegenwart (Präsens)	*he works, he is working*
present participle	Partizip Präsens	*giving, trying, understanding*
present perfect	Perfekt	*she has worked, she has been working*
pronoun	Pronomen (Fürwort)	*my, mine, myself*
quantifier	Mengenbezeichnung	*some, a lot, every*
question	Frage	*Are you coming?*
question tag	Frageanhängsel	*You're German, aren't you?*
question word	Fragewort	*when, why, where, what, how*
reflexive pronoun	Reflexivpronomen	*myself, yourself, herself*
regular verb	regelmäßiges Verb	*listen - listened - listened*
relative clause	Relativsatz	*The car you can see is mine.*
relative pronoun	Relativpronomen	*The building which is ...*
reported speech	indirekte Rede	*She asked him to sit down.*
short answer	Kurzantwort	*Do you smoke? - No, I don't.*
short form	Kurzform (des Hilfsverbs)	*we've, isn't, can't, hadn't*
simple form	einfache Form	*he speaks, he spoke, he has spoken*
singular	Einzahl	*finger, bed, glass*
spelling	Rechtschreibung	'How do you spell it?'

stative verb	Zustandsverb	*believe, love, contain*
stress	Betonung	*hotel, machine, make-up*
subject	Subjekt	*We sing a song.*
subject question	Frage nach dem Subjekt	*Who called this afternoon?*
subordinate clause	Nebensatz	*We are late because …*
superlative	Superlativ	*the cleverest, the most dangerous*
tense	Tempus	*past tense, present tense*
time	Zeit	*past, present, future*
uncountable noun	nicht zählbares Substantiv	*advice, information, chewing gum*
verb	Verb (Zeitwort)	*be, go, play*
vowel	Vokal (Selbstlaut)	*a, e, i, o, u*
word order	Wortstellung	*He (1) arrived (2) at work (3) at ten o'clock (4).*
yes/no question	Entscheidungsfrage	*Was she here? Yes, she was.*

Register (Index)

(Seitenzahlen in **Fettdruck** verweisen auf Schwerpunktkapitel)

a 8
a bit of 8
a few 26
a little 26, 28
a lot of 26
a piece of 8
adjectives **28**, 30, 106, 108
Adjektive **28**, 30, 106, 108
Adverbien 18, **30**, 56
Adverbien der Häufigkeit 30, 56
adverbs 18, **30**, 56
American English (AE) 50, **112**, 114, 116
amerikanisches Englisch 50, **112**, 114, 116
an 8
an item of 8
Antwort 52, 116
any 26
Apostroph 16
Artikel, bestimmt **10**, 112
Artikel, unbestimmt **8**, 14
as 8, 32
auxiliaries **34**, **36**, **38**, **40**, **42**, **44**, 46, **48**, 102
auxiliary substitutes **46**
bad 28
be s. *'to be'*
Bedingungssätze **90**, 102, 110
britisches Englisch 50, 112, 114, 116
British English (BE) 50, 112, 114, 116
by 82
can 36, 38, 46
compounds 26
concession clause 106, 108, 110
conjunctions **32**, 106, 108, 110
could 36, 38, 92
dare 48, 102
date **116**
Datum **116**
defining relative clause 24, 98
definite article **10**, 112
demonstrative pronouns **22**
Demonstrativpronomen **22**
diary future 80
do s. *'to do'*
don't have to 42, 46
don't need to 42, 46
don't want to 40
du 18
dynamische Verben 72
each 26
each other 20
einfache Form der Gegenwart 54, **56**, 74, 80, 82, 90, 94
einfache Form der Vergangenheit 54, **60**, 82, 90, 94, 112
einfache Form der Vorvergangenheit 34, 54, **68**, 82, 90, 94
einfache Form der Zukunft 40, 54, 76
einfache Form des Perfekts 54, **64**, 82, 94, 112
Einräumungssatz 106, 108, 110
Einzahl 12, 14, 16, 36
Ersatzformen für Hilfsverben **46**
every 26
fast 30
Finalsatz 110
for 64, 66, 76, 102
Frage 34, 36, 48, 50, **52f.**, 56, 58, 60, 62, 64, 66, 68, 70, 78, 96
Frageanhängsel **52f.**
Fragepronomen **22**
Fragewort 80, 96
frequency adverbs 30, 56
future 'will' 94
future 'will have' 94
future continuous 54, 76
future forms **74**, **76**, 78
future perfect continuous 34, 54, 76
future perfect simple 34, 54, 76
future simple 40, 54, 76

Gegenwart, einfache Form 54, **56**, 74, 80, 82, 90, 94
Gegenwart, Verlaufsform 54, **58**, 74, 80, 82, 94
Gegenwartsformen für Zukunftsereignisse 74, **80**
Genitiv **16**
genitive **16**
gerade 62
gerund 88, **100**, **104**
Gerund 88, **100**, **104**
going to 74, **78**
going to-future 78
good 28, 30
Grundzahlen **114**
had ('d) better 48
hard 30
hardly 30
Häufigkeitsadverbien 30, 56
Hauptsatz 32, 110
have s. *'to have'*
he 18
her, hers, herself 18, 20
Hilfsverben **34**, **36**, **38**, **40**, **42**, **44**, 46, **48**, 102
Hilfsverben, modal **36**, **38**, **40**, **42**, **44**, 46, 102
Hilfverben, primär **34**
him, himself 18, 20
Hintergrundhandlung 62
his 20
I 18
I wish **92**
if 32, 90, 96, 102, 110
If-Sätze **90**, 102, 110
if-sentences **90**, 102, 110
indefinite article **8**, 14
indirect speech 68, **94**, **96**
Indirekte Rede 68, **94**, **96**
Infinitiv 36, 74, 76, 78, 84, 88, 90, 92, 96, **102f.**, **104**
infinitive 36, 74, 76, 78, 84, 88, 90, 92, 96, **102f.**, **104**
ing-Form 58, 62, 66, 70, 76, 100, 106
interrogative pronouns **22**
Inversion s. ,Umstellung'
it, its, itself 18, 20
kaum 30
Kausalsatz 106, 108, 110
Kettenhandlung 60
Kleidungsstücke 14
Komparativ 28
Konjunktionen **32**, 106, 108, 110
Konsonant 8, 12
Konzessivsatz 106, 108, 110
Kurzantwort **52f.**, 56, 58
Kurzform 18, 34, 50, 68, 116
Länder 12, 14, 16
lassen **84**, 102
let s. *'to let'*
little s. *'a little'*
lots of 26
main clause 32, 110
man 18, 82
many 26
may 36, 38, 46
me 18
Mehrzahl des Substantivs **12**, **14**, 16
Menge(nangaben) 16, **26**
might 36, 38
mine 20
modal auxiliaries **36**, **38**, **40**, **42**, **44**, 46, 102
modale Hilfsverben **36**, **38**, **40**, **42**, **44**, 46, 102
more, most 28
much 26, 28
multi-word verbs **86**
must 36, 38, 42, 46
mustn't 38, 42, 46
my, myself 20
Nebensätze 32, 102, 106, 108, **110**
need s. *'to need to'*
needn't 42
neutral future 78
neutral 'will' 78
nicht (wahr)? 52
nicht brauchen 46
nicht dürfen 38, 46
nicht müssen 46

non-defining relative clauses 98
not s. ‚Verneinung'
numbers **114f.**
oder? 52
of-genitive 16
one another 20
oneself 20
Ordnungszahlen 115
Ort(sangaben) 12, 16, 24, 30, 96
ought to 48
ourselves 20
Partizip Perfekt 36, 44, 64, 68, 76, 82, 84, 90, **108**
Partizip Präsens 36, **106**
Passiv 34, **82f.**, 108
passive 34, **82f.**, 108
past continuous 54, **62**, 82, 94
past participle 36, 44, 64, 68, 76, 82, 84, 90, **108**
past perfect continuous 54, **70**, 94
past perfect simple 34, 54, **68**, 82, 90, 94
past simple 54, **60**, 82, 90, 94, 112
Perfekt, einfache Form 54, **64**, 82, 94, 112
Perfekt, Verlaufsform 54, **66**, 94
personal pronouns **18**
Personalpronomen **18**
Personen 14, 16, 18, 22, 24
phrasal verbs **86**
plural of nouns **12**, **14**, 16
possessive pronouns **20**
Possessivpronomen **20**
Präpositionen 22, **32**, 82, 88, 100, 112
pre-verb adverbs 56
prepositions 22, **32**, 82, 88, 100, 112
present continuous 54, **58**, 74, 80, 82, 94
present-future 78
present participle 36, **106**
present perfect 34, 54, **64**, **66**, 82, 94, 112
present perfect continuous 54, **66**, 94
present perfect simple 54, **64**, 82, 94, 112
present simple 54, **56**, 74, 80, 82, 90, 94
present tense forms for future events 74, **80**
primary auxiliaries **34**
Pronomen **18**, **20**, **22**, **24**, 86, 96, 98
Pronomen der Gegenseitigkeit **20**
pronouns **18**, **20**, **22**, **24**, 86, 96, 98
purpose clause 110
quantifiers 16, **26**
question **52f.**
question tag **52f.**
reason clause 110
reciprocal pronouns **20**
reflexive pronouns **20**
Reflexivpronomen **20**
relative clauses 24, **98**, 106, 108, 110
relative pronouns **24**, 98
Relativpronomen **24**, 98
Relativsätze 24, **98**, 106, 108, 110
s-genitive 16
Sachen 16, 18, 22, 24
selbst 20
several 26
shall 36, 40
she 18
shop apostrophe 16
short answer **52f.**
should 36, 40, 48
Sie 18
since 32, 64, 66, 76
some 14, 26
spontaneous 'will' 78
Sprechabsichten 36, 38, 40
stative verbs **72**
Steigerung 28
subclauses 32, 102, 106, 108, **110**
Substantiv, Mehrzahl **12**, **14**, 16
Substantiv, nicht zählbar 8, 14
Superlativ 28
Temporalsatz 106, 108, 110
Tempus 54
tense 54
that 22, 24, 32, 88, 98, 102f.
that-Satz 88, 102f.
the 10, 28
their, theirs 20
them, themselves 18, 20
there 20, 34
these 22
they 18

this 22
those 22
Tiere 16, 18
time 54, **116**
time clause 110
timetable future 80
to be 8, 18, 34, 56, 58, 60, 62, 66, 70, 76, 78, 82, 108
to be able to 46
to be allowed to 46
to be used to 104
to become 8, 28
to do 34, 50, 52, 60
to get 28
to have 18, 34, 36, 42, 44, **50**, 60, 64, 66, 68, 70, 84, 112
to have got **50**, 112
to have sth done 84
to have to 46
to let 84, 102
to let sb do sth 84
to make sb do sth 84
to need to 48
Uhrzeit **116**
Umstellung 36, 52, 56, 58, 60, 62, 64, 66, 68, 70, 78
unregelmäßige Verben 60, **133ff.**
us 18
used to 48, 104
verb forms **54**
verb patterns **88**
Verben 34, 36, 38, 40, 42, 44, 46, 48, 50, 72, 84, 86, 88
Verben, dynamisch 72
Verben, unregelmäßig 60, **133ff.**
Verben, zusammengesetzt **86**
Verbformen **54**
Vergangenheit, einfache Form 54, **60**, 82, 90, 94, 112
Vergangenheit, Verlaufsform 54, **62**, 82, 94
Verlaufsform der Gegenwart 54, **58**, 74, 80, 82, 94
Verlaufsform der Vergangenheit 54, **62**, 82, 94
Verlaufsform der Vorvergangenheit 54, **70**, 94
Verlaufsform der Zukunft 54, 76
Verlaufsform des Perfekts 54, **66**, 94
Verneinung 34, 36, 50, 56, 58, 60, 62, 64, 66, 68, 70, 78
Vokal 8, 12
Vorvergangenheit, einfache Form 34, 54, **68**, 82, 90, 94
Vorvergangenheit, Verlaufsform 54, **70**, 94
want 40
we 18
Werkzeuge 14
what 22
when 32
where 24
whether 32, 96
which 22, 24, 98
while 32
who(m) 22, 24, 98
whose 22, 24
will 36, 40, 74, 76, **78**, 90, 94
will have 94
will nicht 40
will not (won't) 40
Wortzusammensetzungen 26
would 36, 40, 90, 92, 94
would ('d) rather 48, 102
would have 90, 94
wouldn't 40
you 18
your, yours, yourself, yourselves 20
Zahlen **114f.**
Zeit(angaben) 10, 12, 16, 30, 80, 96, 116
Zeitverschiebung 94, 96
zero if-sentences 90
Zukunft, einfache Form 40, 54, 76
Zukunft, Verlaufsform 54, 76
Zukunftsformen **74**, **76**, 78
Zustandsverben **72**